C000182398

LONDON'S
MARKETS

Andrew Kershman

London's Markets

Written by Andrew Kershman
Photographs by Andrew Kershman
Illustrations by Lesley Gilmour
Book design by Susi Koch and Lesley Gilmour
Edited by David Swindells

Published in 2018 by
Metro Publications
PO Box 6336
London
N1 6PY

Printed and bound in China. This book is produced using paper from registered sustainable and managed sources.

© 2018 Andrew Kershman
British Library Cataloguing in Publication Data.
A catalogue record for this book is available from the British Library.

ISBN: 978-1-902910-60-4

In memory of my Mum, Joy Wright
(1931-2007)

Acknowledgements

I want to thank all my colleagues at Metro for their help and patience. Lesley Gilmour has done a great job making the maps clear and attractive and Susi Koch deserves special thanks for all her help and support designing the book, choosing the photos and providing valuable advice. My editor, David Swindells, has also done a sterling job of correcting my clumsy words and undertaking the laborious task of fact checking.

It's taken over a year to visit all the markets of London and in that time I've met some great people who have been kind enough to provide me with quotes and pose for my pictures. There are too many of these stalwart market people to name here, but they have all helped make this book what it is. Special thanks also go to Markymarket, who allowed me to accompany him on his early morning trawl of Smithfield and Billingsgate. The people who run the markets have also been a great help; including Cheryl Cohen and the team at London's Farmers' Markets, Caron at Duck Pond Markets and Christian for all her help with the review for Flea @ Flat Iron Square.

Contents

Introduction

This book is intended as a snapshot of London's markets over the year it has taken to research and write. I wish for the sake of convenience that everything would remain unchanged and my work would always be accurate, but London's markets are forever in a state of flux. This was made clear at Brick Lane which required several visits. Each time I returned something had moved or changed, so I needed to tread a fine line between giving enough detail to help the reader, while not being too specific and dating the book. I hope I've achieved this balance, but if the man playing chess for free on the corner of Brick Lane and Cheshire Street decides to move his pitch or goes on his hols, I hope you won't feel too resentful – I'm sure you'll agree he was worth mentioning.

The one piece of advice I would give readers is to go a little out of your comfort zone and the markets you already know. This guide gives considerable space to all the famous markets like Portobello, Camden and Borough, but spare a thought for the other 80 or so London markets that you have never heard of but which can be great fun to discover, and are often cheaper than their more famous rivals. Coming back with a sack full of fresh veg from Queen's Market in East Ham for just a tenner or finding an unusual framed oil painting at Douglas flea market – these are some of the pleasant surprises of the last year of research.

London's markets have faced hard times over recent years and the traditional market is certainly suffering from a change in buying habits. The good news is there are many new markets springing up in the capital and the growing popularity of places like Broadway in East London and Borough Market in Bermondsey, alongside a whole host of new vintage fairs and pop-up events, is a sure sign that London's markets are destined to be here for many years to come.

Andrew Kershman

Central

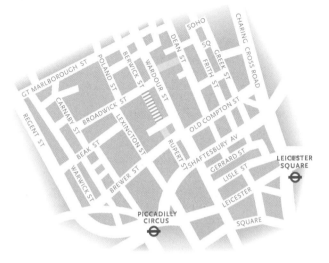

Berwick Street Market

Berwick Street, from Broadwick Street to Peter Street, W1F 8ST
Twitter: @BerwickStMarket
Tube: Oxford Circus (Victoria, Central, Bakerloo), Piccadilly Circus
(Bakerloo, Piccadilly), Tottenham Court Road
(Northern, Central)
Open: Monday-Saturday 8am-5pm

Berwick Street Market is one of London's oldest, dating its origins back to a charter granted by James II over three hundred years ago. The market has faced many ups and downs since that time and its focus on fresh fruit and veg has been lost, with just a few of the traditional traders still selling their great-value produce. Jim's Fruit & Veg is still trading from his usual pitch – although not crying out the latest offerings as they did in former times.

Ronnie's Flowers is another stalwart of the market still going strong after 56 years of trading and now run by Ronnie's daughter. There is another flower stall at the Broadwick Street end of the market which is also worth having a look at for cut flowers and cheap potted plants. The stall that is not to be missed is the *Soho Dairy*, run by the ebullient Robin, and selling unpasteurised cheese and milk and fresh eggs. He has taken on a good deal of the battle with Westminster Council, who for over ten years refused to issue permanent licences to trade. The battle has now been won and not only has the street been pedestrianised – making it a much nicer place to shop and stroll – but permanent licences have been granted to sixteen traders, so securing Berwick Street's future.

The real pull for this market these days are the street food takeaways which are buzzing with hungry workers looking to enjoy a good-value al fresco lunch. In this small stretch you can find food from around the world including Indian, Greek, Middle-Eastern and Thai, with one stall calling itself *Savage Salads* doing a roaring lunchtime trade. The falafel stall is also popular and offers some of the freshest of these Middle-Eastern delicacies to be found in the capital.

Berwick Street is now one of the last remaining central London markets and one well worth exploring if you're in Soho and it is now complemented by Street Food Union, just the other side of Shaftesbury Avenue (see page 45).

Eat & Drink

There are of course lots of street food stalls here, but if your fancy a sit down *My Place* (21 Berwick Street) and *Flat White* (17 Berwick Street) are great places to relax, grab a bite and both serve good coffee.

Visit

Among the attractions of Berwick Street is *Reign Vintage* at number 12 which is great for unique vintage fashion. Lovers of comics and graphic books should look out for *Gosh Comics* on the corner with Peter Street at 1 Berwick Street.

Cabbages & Frocks

St Marlebone Parish Church,
Marylebone High Street, W1U 5BA
www.cabbagesandfrocks.co.uk
Twitter: @cabbagesfrocks
Tube: Baker Street (Circle, Metropolitan, Jubilee, Bakerloo)
Open: Saturday 11am-5pm

This market started life in Hampstead before moving to the grand courtyard of St Marylebone Parish Church in 2006. In this tranquil space around forty stalls can trade, offering a reasonable choice of prepared foods, clothing, accessories and jewellery.

The organisers have ensured the market looks attractive with white canvas awnings arranged around the church's vast horse chestnut tree and several large banners outside advertising the market to passersby. This area is one of the most expensive in London and the stalls that tend to thrive here are those

specialising in vintage or unique new jewellery and the few traders in pre-owned designer clothing and accessories which tend to attract the wealthy bargain-hunting locals and tourist trade. While things can be a little quiet here on an off day, there are plenty of special market events such as summer dog shows and Christmas fairs which attract large crowds and are when this market can be seen at its best.

Eat & Drink

Marylebone High Street has lots of good cafés and eateries, but my favourite is *Bonne Bouche* at 2-3 Thayer Street.

Visit

If you like second-hand shopping Marylebone High Street has a lot of good charity shops. For culture there is the unique and wonderful Wallace Collection, just a few minutes walk away on Manchester Square.

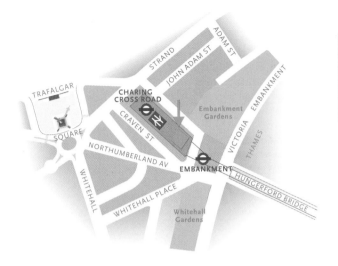

Charing Cross Collectors' Fair

Under Charing Cross Arches, WC2N 5DE
(end of Northumberland Avenue)
www.charingcrossmarket.com
Twitter: @charingmarket
Tube: Embankment (Northern, Bakerloo, District and Circle)
Rail: Charing Cross
Open: Saturday 8am-3pm

Every Saturday a small group of dedicated collectors congregate in this unprepossessing underground car park in central London. Among the thirty or so stalls are specialists in military medals, coins, stamps, bank notes, postcards, cigarette cards and even phone cards. To the uninitiated, collecting things can seem a dull, rather unexciting pastime and the initial impression when entering this concrete bunker will probably confirm this view.

A brief wander among the stalls, however, is sure to unearth something of interest. The coins on display are a good first stop because of their intrinsic appeal. The neatly written labels give details of the type and age of the coin and the dealers are usually willing to expound at length if you want to know more. I was surprised that some coins of considerable antiquity were so cheap.

An English half groat dating from 1461 could be bought here for £16, a Roman denarius for £23 and a Syrian coin from 142 BC for only £12. Other coins of various denominations and ages were piled in great heaps for only a few pence each. It is here that I discovered that my only family heirloom (a 1965 Crown coin commemorating Winston Churchill) was worth the princely sum of 60p. Not all the coins are cheap and some serious collectors spend a good deal of money at the market.

There are many stamp dealers here and experienced collectors spend some time pawing the catalogues with a magnifying glass and tweezers looking for something to add to their collection. It is possible to start a collection for only a few pence but in some instances whole collections are for sale. I asked one bearded, cardigan-clad stall-holder the value of his most expensive stamp, but my question was clearly a crass one for his brow creased as he explained that he didn't think about his collection in that way and then generously volunteered the figure of £75 to help me.

The postcard stalls are a little more accessible to the first-time visitor. They are usually arranged by country or area, but in some cases by subject and are fascinating not only for the vintage pictures on the front but often for the handwritten messages found on the back, addressed to long-deceased correspondents. Although not a collector, I was tempted by the notion of owning a fragment of history for only a few pounds.

Charing Cross Collectors' Fair is a fascinating place to visit and a real culture shock for anyone unfamiliar with the arcane world of collectiing. The original founder of the market back in the 1970s was the inimitable Rodney Bolwell, but he has now retired and his daughter Bridget has taken over the market and is attempting to encourage younger visitors with special discounts and the launching of a basic but useful website. Let's hope the next generation can get involved and keep this unique event running for another forty years.

Eat & Drink

The Collectors' Fair is located in the centre of town and is surrounded by cafés, restaurants and pubs. My favourite is the café in the Embankment Garden which is just the other side of Charing Cross Station.

Visit

There are many places to visit after a morning at the Collectors' Fair, including The National Portrait Gallery, The National Gallery and The Southbank Centre which always has a busy programme of events and concerts and also features a great book market under Waterloo Bridge (see page 39). The Embankment Gardens extend along the north bank of the Thames and are wonderful places to visit when the weather is fine.

Covent Garden

Covent Garden Piazza, WC2H 7AR
www.coventgarden.london/markets
Tube: Covent Garden (Piccadilly)
Open: Tuesday-Saturday 10.30am-6pm (arts & crafts)
Monday 10.30am-6pm (antiques & collectables)

These days the pedestrianised streets around Covent Garden
piazza are thronged with tourists enjoying the shopping and the
licensed street performers. The Georgian lamps in the piazza
with their pineapple motifs and the black and white photos of
former traders in the passageways, all tell the story of Covent
Garden's long history as a wholesale fruit, veg and flower market.
Covent Garden was first granted a royal charter by Charles II in
1670. In 1973 this rough-and-ready working market moved to a
modern complex in Nine Elms near Vauxhall and the old Piazza
opened as a shopping and entertainment area in 1980.

The market is now a very small part of Covent Garden with only one avenue within the Piazza (the Apple Market) and the Jubilee Hall, just to the south of the square, dedicated to market trading. The Apple Market has about 50 stalls selling antiques and collectables on Mondays and arts and crafts during the rest of the week. There are some interesting things to be found here with wooden toys, clocks, clothing and accessories all well presented and commanding high prices. The crafts market also has quite a few jewellery designers selling their contemporary creations, many of whom accept individual commissions.

Next to the London Transport Museum is the Jubilee Market which is larger than the Apple Market, but housed in a less attractive modern building. The items for sale tend to be a little more tourist orientated with small pub signs, heraldic symbols and Union Jack T-shirts all on display during the week. As well as the novelty items there are also a few stalls offering practical things like cheap bags and street fashion which are worth a look. At the back of the market, facing onto Tavistock Street, is *Doolittle's* flower stall which has been here for years and is a throw back to the time when this place was dedicated to flora.

Covent Garden Market is really at its best on Mondays when both the Apple and Jubilee Market are dedicated to antiques and collectables, offering anything from piles of junk jewellery for a £1 an item to attractive displays of genuine collectables bearing a much higher price tag. The Jubilee Hall is a popular feature of London's antiques business with several traders from Bermondsey and Camden Passage also trading here on a Monday. The place is well worth a visit if you are in search of an unusual gift or just want to enjoy the quirky atmosphere, with lots of regulars showing up here to pass the time and occasionally haggle over a particular item that has caught their fancy. Take a few minutes to look at the plaque on the side of Jubilee Hall, on the corner of Southampton Street, which gives a brief account of the market's illustrious history.

Visit

There are numerous attractions in and around Covent Garden, the most prominent being The London Transport Museum (right next to the market). Street performers are a popular feature of Covent Garden with acrobats, dancers and opera singers plying their trade. Those interested in architecture should take a look at St Paul's Church to the west of the Piazza which was designed by Inigo Jones. Just ten minutes walk away, on Trafalgar Square, is The National Gallery and The National Portrait Gallery.

Earlham Street

Earlham Street between Shaftesbury Avenue and
Seven Dials, WC2H 9HW
Tube: Leicester Square (Northern and Piccadilly);
Covent Garden (Piccadilly)
Open: Monday-Saturday 11am-7.30pm This quaint street, just
next to Cambridge Circus, hosts one of London's most central
markets. The market has, however, been affected by disruptive
renovation work in recent years and has dwindled to just a
handful of stalls offering street food, women's fashion and an
excellent stall specialising in hats, sunglasses and accessories.
The market is small, but occasionally a great value fashion trader
will show up here, making it worth a visit if you're passing. The
workmen and their drills and lorries have gone, leaving Earlham
Street looking very smart and hopefully signalling the revival of
this special market.

Central

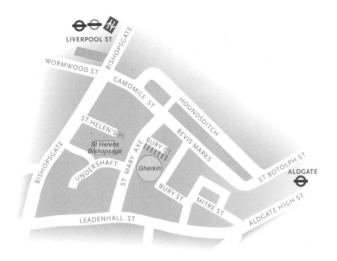

KERB Gherkin

30 St Mary Axe, EC3A 8EP

www.kerbfood.com/gherkin

Tube: Aldgate (Circle, Metropolitan), Liverpool Street (Central, Circle, Hammersmith & City)

Rail: Liverpool Street

Open: Thursday 12noon-2pm

On Thursdays the hard working City folk of the square mile get a brief but flavourful visitation from KERB. A line-up of eight fantastic street food specialists set up here offering anything from wholemeal pitta wraps to meaty burgers and fries. The traders change from week to week so check out their website for a heads-up on the current line-up. For more KERB markets see Camden Lock (page 76) and King's Cross (page 101).

Leather Lane

Leather Lane, EC1N 7TS
(between Clerkenwell Road and Greville Street)
www.leatherlanestars.wordpress.com
Tube: Farringdon (Circle and Metropolitan),
Chancery Lane (Central)
Open: Monday-Friday 10.30am-2.00pm

For years Leather Lane stood as a fine example of a general
weekday market providing groceries and household goods to the
locals of Clerkenwell. There are still remnants of that atmosphere
and local charm, but recently many of the market's old characters
have left, including the well-known stall at the top of the market
selling discounted magazines. In their place have arrived street
food businesses offering food from around the globe and drawing
a hungry lunch time crowd.

The range of food here and the number of food stalls is remarkable and includes Indian curries, Thai food provided by *Yum Bowl* (also on Whitecross Street), and the Caribbean jerk chicken stall which is a favourite with the local shop workers in search of some spicy protein on their lunch break. The Korean fast food stall has long queues and plenty of regulars coming back for more. Further along a stall specialising in vegan food makes delicious lentil wraps with salad. Of course, before all the street food arrived there was always a much loved baked potato van and it is still here and still serving up delicious slow baked potatoes with plenty of fillings.

The change in style has left some of the more traditional stalls a bit surprised. Lisa has been selling bags on the street for 27 years and wanders what's happened:

> *"You can now get all types of food here, but you can't buy much clothing. Everyone wants to eat and no one wants to buy anything anymore; they get that kind of stuff online these days."*

With a cheerful smile and a shrug she goes about her business, tidying her stock and waiting for some last minute trade before packing away.

The flower stall run by Louise and her partner is another established business offering great value cut flowers and a small selection of healthy looking pot plants. Her cucumber plants for just a few quid are popular with the local Indian shoppers who love to grow and eat there own fresh vegetables. Further along is one of the few surviving fruit and veg stalls. It's run by Michael, who after university and an office job, took over the stall from his grandfather. After 15 years here he still enjoys it and even loves the street food and the new traders who regularly give him a free lunch, which is often rewarded with some veg 'on the house'. At the far end of the market is a small square where most of the clothing is now concentrated. The emphasis here is on cheap street fashion and there are plenty of good quality bargains to be found with few items over £10. Another regular at this part of the market is the cheap packaged food stall with lots of biscuits, sweets and tinned foods. It's a comfort to see a few of the old style stalls still here; let's hope they can continue.

Central

Lower Marsh

Lower Marsh Street, SE1 7RG

www.wearewaterloo.co.uk/market

Twitter: @LowerMarshMrkt

Tube: Waterloo, Lambeth North (Northern)

Rail: Waterloo (take the exit nearest Platform 1, follow the road down and take the underpass into Leake Street)

Open: Monday-Friday 10am-5pm (street food and general); Saturdays 10am-5pm (general flea market with arts and crafts)

For over 150 years Lower Marsh has hosted a vibrant weekday market, but by the mid noughties it had dwindled to just a few stalls. Things needed to change and in recent years the market has been given a new lease of life during the week with a far greater emphasis on street food which brings in the local office workers for a cheeky al fresco lunch, while on Saturdays the market offers a mix of general arts and crafts and vintage goods.

The weekday market is now dominated by street food stalls offering anything from Thai curry to slow-cooked BBQ ribs and these stalls are always busy during the lunch-time rush. There are quite a few other stalls here during the week including one specialising in cacti, a picture framers, a stall offering cheap street fashion and the toiletries and cosmetics pitch run by Barry, who has been trading here for over 20 years, making him the old timer on the street.

The atmosphere at the weekend is relaxed with lots of stalls offering great value cakes, vintage clothing, street fashion, house plants, jewellery and even a second-hand book stall. One of the most interesting Saturday stalls is that run by *Johnny Skates* who has an incredible stock of vinyl and always has a crowd of cool music fanatics in search of something to add to their collection.

Lower Marsh Street Market has adapted to what consumers want and although some might regret the changes, the market team responsible (*We Are Waterloo*) have improved things. It seems that this charming little street behind Waterloo Station will have a market for many years to come.

Eat & Drink

There's a great deal of street food here but also some great cafés including the award winning *Four Corners Café*, *Coleman Coffee Roasters*, the more old school *Marie's Café* and the *Camel & Artichoke* which is a good place for a pint.

Visit

Travelling Through (131 Lower Marsh) is a great independent bookshop. Further afield there is plenty to explore, with the Southbank Centre and the London Eye within walking distance. Petrol heads should visit on the third Saturday of the month when the street is the venue for *Waterloo Classics* (www. waterlooclassics.com) with lots of classic British cars on display.

Piccadilly Market

St James's Churchyard, W1J 9LL
www.piccadilly-market.co.uk
Twitter: @piccadillymart
Tube: Piccadilly Circus (Piccadilly)
Open: Monday-Tuesday 11am-5pm (food),
Wednesday-Saturday 10am-6pm (arts and crafts)

St James's Church has played host to a market for many decades
with the old trees and ancient stone paving remaining constant
while the people and the merchandise sold have gradually
changed over the years. These days the churchyard is given over
to a vibrant street food market on Mondays and Tuesdays offering
food from around the world for as little as £5 a go and plenty of
shaded benches in the church grounds to eat in comfort.

From Wednesday to Saturday Piccadilly takes on its more
established role as an arts and crafts market, offering anything

from tourist novelties to genuine antiques. One of the most interesting stalls is run by Linda who has been selling her antique glassware and tableware at the market for years and loves the people and the place. Other stalls offer leather belts and bags, wooden toys, hand painted glass, brightly painted plates in a Greek style, jewellery, kids' clothes and quite a few stalls catering to the passing tourist trade with toy red buses, tiny models of Big Ben and Union Jack T-shirts all to the fore. The tourist stuff might deter some, but there are good things to be found here and the tranquil atmosphere is a welcome break from the bustle of Piccadilly which lies beyond the church gates.

Eat & Drink

There are lots of options for refreshment during the street food market, but when the Craft Market takes place your best bet is the *Caffè Nero* that lies within the church grounds.

Visit

St James's Church is a fine one and well worth exploring. Art lovers should also take the opportunity to visit The Royal Academy which is just opposite, on the north side of Piccadilly.

Smithfield

Charterhouse Street, EC1A 9PS
www.smithfieldmarket.com
Tube: Farringdon or Barbican (Circle, Metropolitan,
Hammersmith & City)
Rail: Farringdon
Open: Monday-Friday 2am-12noon

Meat has been sold at Smithfield Market for over eight hundred
years and it is now the last wholesale market in London to remain
on its original site. The present building is an impressive edifice
of iron, stone and brick, designed by Sir Horace Jones (who
also designed Leadenhall Market) and built in 1866. Behind the
immutable exterior, however, things have not stayed still and the
market underwent a £70 million redevelopment in the 1990s.

If you walk through the central archway at the bottom of St John
Street and take a look down any of the buyers' avenues the change is

easy to see. The interior of the massive Victorian building has been stripped out and, instead of the rather dark chaotic workings of the old market, new avenues have been created with each trader selling meat from modern counters with the produce being unpacked behind glass screens directly from the lorries. These changes were primarily introduced to improve efficiency and conform to hygiene regulations, but they also make this a far more welcoming place for members of the public to shop, if also diminishing some of the market's spit and sawdust vitality.

The best time to visit the market is very early in the morning (around 2am) when the larger lorries are just beginning to leave having deposited their stock and a small army of white transit vans clog the streets ready to collect their wares for distribution around the capital. This part of the city (near Farringdon) is also a major nightclub area with young crowds queuing outside *Fabric* in full party mode, while Smithfield's porters in their white outfits go about their business. Although a lot of the trade here in the early morning is commercial, private customers are welcomed and the staff are generally helpful – although not averse to a bit of banter and some gentle teasing when the mood takes them. If you can't make it to the market at this early hour the place is still trading through until lunchtime, although the best cuts have by then been sold. Another option is to employ the services of Markymarket (www.markymarket.com / Twitter @markymarket), who visits both Smithfield and Billingsgate Markets several times a week and delivers straight to your door.

Eat & Drink

The Hope (94 Cowcross Street), *Fox and Anchor* (115 Charterhouse Street) are great pubs, both of which open from 7am for the market trade. If you're going later in the day there are lots of eateries on Cowcross Street to explore.

Southbank
Book Market

Riverside Walk under Waterloo Bridge in front of the BFI, SE1 8XX
Tube/Rail: Waterloo (Northern)
Open: Daily 12noon-6pm (winter); 11am-7pm (summer)
It would be hard to imagine a more perfect location for a book
market than on the south bank of the Thames, just outside the
British Film Institute (BFI), under the protection of Waterloo
Bridge and with a fantastic view of the London skyline. Not only is
Southbank Book Market a good place to browse for books but, with
a broad tree-lined pedestrian 'boulevard', it also has a romantic
atmosphere. I am not alone in thinking this – it was here that Hugh
Grant made his declaration of love in the film *Four Weddings and
a Funeral* and I know of one couple that carried out a good deal of
their courtship here. The secret of the place is that, although it is in

the centre of London, its' spirit and atmosphere is reminiscent of the banks of the Seine. After only a few minutes of browsing among the books I feel the urge to don a black polo neck, start smoking Gitanes and buy at least one book about existentialism.

The market has eight regular traders who set out about sixty tables, heaving under the weight of thousands of books covering most subjects. Works by all the giants of European and American literature can be found here including such names as Dickens, Balzac, Henry James, Orwell, Steinbeck and Kafka. If you prefer a good page-turner there are enough books by the likes of Dan Brown, Stieg Larsson and Stephanie Meyer to keep you entertained. This is also a good market to visit for academic and reference books with plenty of philosophy, psychology, art history and architecture.

Naturally, being in the heart of the recently modernised Southbank Centre there is a good selection of screenplays and books about film and theatre. Biographies are also well represented with anything from Kitty Kelly's prurient treatment of Frank Sinatra to more noble attempts to capture the lives of novelist Graham Greene or movie star Greta Garbo. If the market cannot supply what you're looking for traders are always willing to give advice. Three of the book sellers have been here since the market's foundation in 1983, so there is a good deal of well-read and experienced help on hand if needed. In recent years there has been an increase in the number of prints, posters, maps and modern art work on sale, with one trader only specialising in these things.

The Southbank Book Market is not the cheapest place to find second-hand books, with most paperbacks selling for around half their new price, but among the thousands of books on offer you can usually find the odd bargain. Anyway most of the people visiting here are really interested in enjoying the atmosphere and having a browse, rather than merely trying to save a few quid.

Eat & Drink

The *BFI Bar & Kitchen* is right next to the market and the *National Theatre* café is just across the boulevard. Further west, along the Thames, are several cafés and restaurants housed within the Southbank Centre including the fabulous *Queen Elizabeth Roof Garden Bar*, which is a great place to relax on fine days.

Visit

The Southbank Centre offers art at the Hayward Gallery, classical and contemporary concerts and dance performances at the Royal Festival and Queen Elizabeth Halls, and art cinema and the annual London Film Festival at the BFI. The centre is also home to *Foyles* bookshop which is worth visiting if the market has not slated your appetite for books.

Central

Southbank Centre Food Market

Behind the Southbank Centre,
Belvedere Road, SE1 8XX
www.southbankcentre.co.uk/book-market
Twitter: @SCFoodMarket
Tube/Rail: Waterloo (Northern and Bakerloo)
Open: Friday 12noon-8pm, Saturday 11am-8pm,
Sunday 12noon-6pm, Bank holiday Mondays 12noon-6pm
Just behind the concrete edifice of the Southbank Centre is a
relatively quiet square which is easily missed by those enjoying
a walk along the Thames, but from Friday to Sunday this is
definitely a place to seek out as it transforms itself into a culinary
oasis of street food stalls. The place isn't that hard to find – just
follow the delicious aroma of cooking.

About 60 stalls set up here serving anything from authentic Polish sausage sandwiches to Katsu Curry and Korean BBQ. There are lots of meaty choices with all kinds of burger combinations, but vegans and vegetarians will also find plenty to make them smile, such as vegan Ethiopian dishes and veggie Indian curry. Those with a sweet tooth should save some space for dessert with quite a few stalls specialising in delicious cakes and pastries and several baristas on hand if you want a coffee. Those seeking something stronger can find anything from artisan beers to cocktails. This market is a real pleasure and definitely worth a visit if you're on the Southbank and feeling peckish.

Visit

The Southbank Centre includes the Hayward Gallery and British Film Institute both of which are worth seeking out. For markets don't forget the Southbank Book Market which is just the other side of the SBC and always has a great selection of books (see page 39).

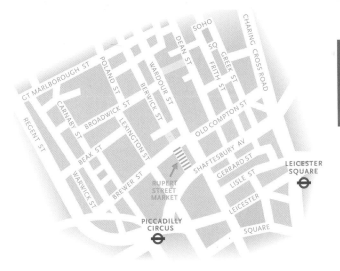

Street Food Union
@ Rupert Street

Rupert Street, W1D 6DS
www.streetfoodunion.com
Tube: Oxford Circus (Victoria, Central), Piccadilly Circus
(Bakerloo, Piccadilly), Tottenham Court Road (Northern, Central),
Leicester Square (Piccadilly, Jubilee)
Open: Monday-Friday 11am-3.30pm
Throughout the week this narrow pedestrian street on the fringes
of Soho is transformed into a hive of culinary activity with about
15 stalls providing delicious food from around the world. The only
problem for visitors is making a decision about what to eat, with
Korean BBQ, Jerk Chicken, Thai and Indian Curry, duck wraps and
even Venezuelan filled rolls among the options. All the menus are
great value with most dishes around a fiver and very few over £7.

The people serving are a friendly, helpful lot and more than willing to explain the menu options if they have the time, although the *Salad Mafia* stall (offering fried chicken and salad) had a long queue with quite a few choosing the veggie option with grilled halloumi. Several of the traders cross national culinary boundaries and none more so than the lads selling a Yorkshire Burrito, which involves using a Yorkshire pud as a burrito – strange, but delicious.

This small street does get busy during the lunchtime rush but there are enough tables and benches to allow customers to sit and enjoy their food – avoiding the need to walk and munch which is often unavoidable at some street food events.

Strutton Ground

Strutton Ground (south side of Victoria Street), SW1P 2JT
Tube: St James's Park (Circle, District)
Rail: Victoria
Open: Monday-Friday 11.30am-3pm

Strutton Ground is a weekday market that is undergoing the kind
of change that has transformed similar markets like Leather Lane
and Whitecross Street into largely street food markets. In the
case of Strutton Ground the process is not yet complete and the
market is divided between the old traders who have been here for
years, selling new and used women's fashion, fruit and veg and a
trader selling discounted foot wear and the new street food stalls
offering all kinds of takeaway food for around a fiver. The market
might be divided evenly between old and new, but it's easy to see
where the money is being made with long queues for the street
food and the traditional traders quiet and understandably glum.

The longest serving stall holder is Ray – the fruit and veg man – who has been trading here for 22 years, but thinks this might be his last:

> *"Everything's changed in the last few years, I don't know the people... I don't feel this is my market anymore. All these new people will queue up for something called 'a kick ass burrito' for a fiver, but they won't pay a few quid for a bag of fresh fruit! I probably won't be here much longer, the way things are going..."*

Further down the market it's not hard to understand Ray's resentment as people queue at the six or seven street food stalls and money is rapidly handed over in exchange for hot boxes of delicious food. The atmosphere at this end of the market is very different with most stalls employing a handful of young energetic people – all of them are working hard to keep up, but also enjoying the experience. There is nothing more up beat than a successful market and nothing sadder than a quiet market and so Strutton Ground is definitely a very divided place at the moment. Let's hope things improve for the more traditional traders and this remains a mixed market, rather than one dominated by street food, however tasty it might be...

"Everything's changed in the last few years, I don't know the people... I don't feel this is my market anymore. All these new people will queue up for something called 'a kick ass burrito' for a fiver, but they won't pay a few quid for a bag of fresh fruit!"

cken & Halloumi S. £6
tra Chicken/Halloumi £6
ble Chicken/Halloumi £1
n of Hummus £2.00

Tachbrook Street

Tachbrook Street between Warwick Way and
Churton Street, SW1V 2JS
Twitter:@TachbrookStMkt
Tube: Pimlico (Victoria), Victoria (Victoria, District and Circle)
Rail: Victoria
Open: Thursday-Saturday 9.30am-5pm

Tachbrook Street market has experienced a slight revival in its
fortunes in recent years. These days about twelve stalls show
up here from Thursday to Saturday. This doesn't sound a lot,
but it includes an excellent fishmongers and butchers as well as
a great-value fruit and veg stall – making it possible for locals to
do a good deal of their weekly shop here, which is rare for a small
market these days. The always popular street food stalls have
found their way onto Tachbrook Street with Thai curry, Moroccan
salads and falafel all represented. At the further end of the market

(towards Churton Street) can be found a useful hardware and household goods stall, which again is a rarity at a local market. Mark's vintage stall is at the far end of the market with a selection of stylish, second-hand clothing, accessories and objects for the home such as lamps and mirrors. Mark has lots of friends and loyal customers and is rarely left to his own devices as people pop by for a chat and to check out his latest stock. Tachbrook Street is a lovely local market, probably not worth going out of your way to visit, but well worth exploring if you're in the Victoria area.

Eat & Drink

Gastronomia Italia is a fantastic deli and café just beyond the market on Tachbrook Street and *Art Tapas* – just opposite on Churton Street – is also a great place to relax and have a coffee.

Visit

If you like hunting for bargains there are several excellent charity shops on Warwick Way and a great vintage store *Pimlico Trove* at 20 Upper Tachbrook Street. Tate Britain is also just a ten-minute walk from here.

Whitecross Street

Whitecross Street between Old Street and Errol Street, EC1Y 8QP
Tube/Rail: Old Street
Open: Monday-Friday 10am-2.30pm

Whitecross Street was a struggling week day market for many years as people changed their shopping habits. To survive the market has certainly undergone a huge transformation in recent years. Peter, who ran the last remaining fruit and veg stall for over 30 years, has gone and in his place have come a vast number of street food stalls and vans, offering food from around the world along this stretch of road that can be traversed in five minutes gentle strolling.

The stylish vintage Citroën van at the Old Street end of the market is run by *Buddha Bowls* who manage to cram streamed seasonal greens, curry, soya chunks, carrot and homemade kimchi pickle all into one fragrant cardboard container for just a fiver.

Further into the market carnivores can get their fill with delicious Turkish kebabs, Katsu chicken and there are even two Swedish lads offering their homeland's famous meatballs with mashed potato. Other continental favourites include a popular French galettes stall and one making authentic Italian pizza to order. Vegans and veggies are further catered for at *Sunny's Olive Tree* which offers all kinds of delicious lunchtime treats.

Those with a sweet tooth will not be disappointed with several traders offering fine patisserie, fresh juices and Jerry's stall selling various kinds of single source honey and nougat bars and a coffee stall with seating on fine days.

There are a few non-food stalls on the market with one lone trader offering household goods and another specialising in jewellery. At the far end of the street market is a privately run covered market with stalls offering bags, cheap street clothing, cards and some really attractive discounted cookbooks. This is where the locals from the nearby estate hunt for bargains but few of the office workers grabbing an al fresco lunch venture down this far.

Traditionalists might not like the change to Whitecross Street, but the hungry crowds and busy food sellers show that this change was necessary. Better a food market than no market at all.

Eat & Drink
There are a few eateries along the road including *The Two Brewers* pub at 121, the old-school *Elite Café* (187) and *Market Restaurant* (132) and *The Iskelé* Turkish restaurant (179-81).

Visit
Whitecross Street is book ended by two arts institutions: The Barbican Centre to the south and to the north, St Luke's is home to the London Symphony Orchestra and offers regular lunchtime concerts.

North

Alexandra Palace Farmers' Market

Campsbourne School, Nightingale Lane, N8 7AF
or Alexandra Palace Park, N22 7AY
www.weareccfm.com
Twitter: @allypallyfm
Rail: Alexandra Park
Open: Sunday 10am-3pm

The farmer's market at Alexandra Palace is one of the largest and most successful markets of its kind in London with over 60 stalls setting out their wares and several thousand loyal customers even on the coldest and wettest of Sundays.

The appeal of the market lies in the diversity and quality of the food and goods on offer. There's a wide choice of fresh organic produce straight from the farm with *Wild Country Organics* being one of the most prominent and popular such producers. There's also a good choice of quality meat with *High Meadows Welsh Farm* offering a tempting selection of their own reared meats and the farmer always on hand to give advice and background to the meat on display. Award winning sausages are also available from *Giggly Pig* with all kinds of meaty flavours from which to choose and discounts for multi-buys. There are quite a few food specialists here with the Portobello Mushroom Man offering the kind of fungi varieties not to be found in an average supermarket, several quality cheese retailers and a very popular fishmonger whose stock tends to run low by midday.

Ally Pally not only caters for the enthusiastic cook but also has a great selection of prepared foods and deli produce. One of best is run by an Italian woman who prepares her own authentic Italian dishes ready to take home and eat, including rich lasagne and deliciously light tiramisu. If you fancy hearty British fare, *Brockley's Pies* are hard to beat, with anything from steak and kidney pies to sweet desserts to take away and enjoy at your leisure. There are plenty of sweet treats here, with Emma (trading as *Life of Pie*) offering a particularly tempting array of her own baked creations.

If all this food has made you peckish, there are plenty of street food traders with the fried fish and calamari stall proving particularly popular. The Indian Curry stall is also a firm favourite with generous servings of curry and rice plus a side dish for just a fiver.

The market is run by *City & County Farmers Markets* who host a number of great markets across the Capital and are not so precious about the concept of a farmers' market as to exclude other kinds of stall. So here you find a charity selling reconditioned furniture and a local ceramicist selling her unique cups and plates which adds to the diversity and appeal of the market. The event alternates between two locations around Alexandra Palace Park, so check on the website before making a special trip.

Alfies Antiques Market

13-25 Church Street, NW8 8DT
www.alfiesantiques.com
Twitter: @AlfiesAntiques
Instagram: alfiesantiques
Tube: Marylebone, Edgware Road (Bakerloo)
Open: Tuesday-Saturday 10am-6pm

Alfies is situated in the midst of Church Street Market (see page 89) and acts as a fascinating contrast with its more down-to-earth neighbour. Within this lofty five-storey Edwardian building there are over 70 dealers selling jewellery, furniture, costume and retro clothing, lighting, tableware, objets d'art, paintings, clocks and books. There are some great items of furniture to inspire a retro revamp from Art Deco chairs to large angle-poise lamps, but you'll need fairly deep pockets to get your hands on such authentic collectables.

If such things are a little beyond your budget there are many traders dealing in attractive but less collectable items with lower price tags. Among these are several good costume jewellery dealers with lots of appealing goodies to sift through for just a few quid.

Several art dealers ply their trade here, but I was particularly drawn to the poster dealer with huge French advertising posters of the 1920s and 30s. A large poster costs several hundred pounds, but then Gallic style is an expensive commodity.

Alfies certainly has a good deal of charm. The dealers are friendly, knowledgeable and occasionally eccentric, the building is huge with numerous staircases and various levels within each storey and there is even an iron staircase with glass roof and a small water feature on the ground floor. Another good thing about Alfies is its diversity with lots of 20th century items as well as the more traditional antiques for which it is better known. Alfies has an excellent roof top café which has a fantastic outdoor terrace with panoramic views of the city across the rooftops.

Archway Market

Navigator Square, N19 3TD
www.archwaymarket.org
Twitter: @ArchwayMarket
Tube: Archway (Northern)
Open: Saturday 10am–5pm

This friendly community market has been around since 2008, but has recently moved to this newly renovated pedestrian avenue. Archway locals have taken the market to their hearts and regularly show up here to enjoy the atmosphere, chat with stall holders and, of course, do a bit of shopping.

Archway may be smaller than some, but it punches above its weight with a great fruit and veg stall offering all kinds of fresh seasonal produce. Artisan cheeses are provided by the fantastic *Cheese Power* stall who sell at a number of markets around the capital and *Marsh Produce* offer a selection of quality, free range meat. There are a few stalls offering bread and pastries with plenty of samples so you can try before you buy. Street food is all the rage at the moment and Archway has a good International choice including Greek souvlaki wraps, Italian croquettes and the ever popular stall offering delicious hog roast sandwiches.

The market also boasts a few interesting bric-à-brac stalls, one of which is run by Barry, who traded for over thirty years in Camden Passage. His stall is a wonderful mix of curiosities and he is always on hand to tell you about his stock, if you're curious. Each week there's a pop-up stall featuring a different local 'maker' with a carpenter, jewellery maker and even a tailor among the regulars. A visit to Archway wouldn't be compete without a browse at the long standing book stall (*Word on the Street*), which always has a great stock of reasonably priced paperback to sift through.

Eat & Drink

There's lots to eat on the market, but if the weather isn't great and you fancy a break, *Ally's Kitchen* is next to the market and does great coffee.

Visit

If you have taken the trouble to travel up to Archway and the weather is fine, you could explore the nearby Archway Park or take a ten minutes walk up Highgate Hill to visit the wonderful Waterlow Park. At the entrance to the park, Lauderdale House hosts regular events and has a café which serves delicious, freshly made food and has outdoor seating. At the other end of the park is the great Highgate Cemetery which is the final resting place of luminaries such as Karl Marx and George Eliot. The cemetery runs regular guided tours which are well worth trying.

Camden Markets

Camden High Road, NW1
www.camdenmarket.com
Twitter: @CamdenMarket
Instagram: CamdenMarketLDN
Tube: Camden Town, Chalk Farm (Northern)
Open: Various times, see each market for details

On the stretch of Camden High Street from Camden Town tube station to Harmood Street there are four separate markets but most people know them collectively as Camden Market. Camden is known throughout Europe as a place of hedonism, fashion and music and this reputation draws vast crowds of teenagers and young adults to the area every weekend. Visiting Camden at its busiest you can see every form of haircut and subculture style from Punks and Goths to the latest complicated creations involving hair extensions. Those with grey hair or a bald pate are a rarity here and the older people that you see are usually anxious parents accompanying their young on a shopping trip. Camden is now dedicated to all the things that youth find interesting with lots of fashion stalls, vinyl dealers, retro clothing, fashion footwear, jewellery and accessories, pot-smoking paraphernalia, posters and lots of tourist souvenirs.

Camden Lock and particularly the Stables Market have been under a process of constant transformation and redevelopment over the last fifteen years and the Stables with its glass office complex and wide stone steps descending to a further subterranean market area is unrecognisable from the ramshackle collection of stalls that started the market back in the mid 1970s. The changes are set to continue and with the market under new ownership there are currently plans for a further £300 million redevelopment of the Stables and Lock Markets that will bring even more change. The upheavals and redevelopments mean little to the crowds of young people from across the world that visit Camden every weekend in search of the fashionable, the unique and the original. Let's hope that with the changes that are to come they won't be disappointed.

Camden Market

Camden High Street, south of Buck Street, NW1 7BT
www.camdenmarket.com
Twitter: @CamdenMarket
Instagram: CamdenMarketLDN
Open: Thursday-Sunday 9am-5.30pm

This small square containing about one hundred stalls is the first outdoor market the crowds encounter after disgorging from Camden tube. It seems to have become a victim of its own success with everything now brought down to the lowest common denominator – and that denominator seems to be the novelty T-shirt. The place is always packed at the weekends with teenagers from around the world brushing shoulders with each other and trying to find anything to buy. There used to be a few stalls that sold original clothing, but they have left and there is now little to choose between the stalls but T-shirts, cheap sunglasses and dope smoking paraphernalia. Teenagers love this place, but those with a mortgage and responsibilities will be appalled. Greenwich, Spitalfields and Portobello Markets are all better options if you're looking for original street fashion.

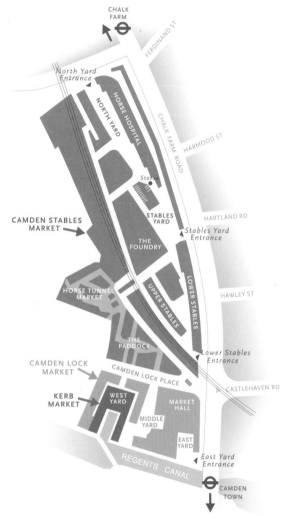

CHALK
FARM

FERDINAND ST

*North Yard
Entrance*

HORSE HOSPITAL

NORTH YARD

CHALK FARM ROAD

HARMOOD ST

Statue

HARTLAND RD

STABLES
YARD

**CAMDEN STABLES
MARKET** →

*Stables Yard
Entrance*

THE
FOUNDRY

LOWER STABLES

HAWLEY ST

**HORSE TUNNEL
MARKET**

UPPER STABLES

THE
PADDOCK

*Lower Stables
Entrance*

**CAMDEN LOCK
MARKET** →

CAMDEN LOCK PLACE

CASTLEHAVEN RD

**KERB
MARKET** →

WEST
YARD

MARKET
HALL

MIDDLE
YARD

EAST
YARD

REGENTS CANAL

*East Yard
Entrance*

CAMDEN
TOWN

Camden Lock Market
Northwest of Camden Lock, Chalk Farm Road, NW1 8AB
www.camdenlockmarket.com
Open: Tuesday-Sunday 10am-6pm, Thursday till 7pm

This part of Camden is at the very heart of the ramshackle market that began here in the 1970's. Over the years it has evolved and now includes a complicated maze of shopping and eating areas.

The East Yard has a glass roof and is one of the last places in Camden where people can get a stall at short notice. Here you will find jewellery, vinyl, some fashion from local designers and a great selection of original T-shirts designs. This part of the market isw scheduled for redevelopment and even the long standing traders don't know how long they will trade on the site.

The Middle Yard is more of a thoroughfare with just a handful of stalls offering kids' clothing and toys, scarves and a specialist in beard care products. The Market Hall contains about 70 stalls on two levels with the emphasis upon arts and crafts. Here you can find colourful hand-painted silk ties, contemporary oil paintings of London life, scented candles, leather-bound note pads, hand-made jewellery and a variety of contemporary bags. There is also a small independent bookshop (*Books Iconica*) which offers quality new books at a discount.

Camden Lock Place is the dividing line between Camden Lock and the vast glass structure that marks the beginning of The Stables Market. This cobbled avenue has a good selection of stalls largely dealing in fashion and ethnic gear, but there is also the *Camera Hut* selling used photographic equipment and another offering Copper water bottles which are supposed to have health giving properties. At the far end of this avenue is *Josiah Amari* where designer Maria makes her own range of kids' wear and will alter and even make bespoke garments to order within an hour. There are lots more food stalls at the other end of the passage including a very popular vegan burger joint.

KERB Camden Lock

Camden Lock Market, NW1 8AF
www.kerbfood.com
Twitter: @KERB_
Instagram: Kerbfood
Monday-Thursday 11am-6pm, Friday-Sunday 11am-7pm

The KERB markets are largely travelling culinary circuses arriving at a venue, turning it into a delicious oasis for as little as a few hours and then packing up and going on their way, leaving nothing but satisfied appetites and epicurean memories. Their market at Camden Lock is a very different beast with 34 traders serving delicious food from around the globe seven days a week.

There's just about every kind of street food to be found here from servings of fresh pasta to pocket kebabs, hefty burgers and fries to vegan curry and tacos. As there's so much choice it's best to have a look around before you choose and the chefs are a friendly bunch with plenty of tasters so you can try before you buy.

Camden Stables Market

West of Chalk Farm Road and Opposite Hartland Road, NW1 8AH
Open: Daily 9am-5pm

The dividing line between the Lock and Camden Stables is now marked by a glass fronted office complex that rises above a maze of shopping avenues lined with permanent units offering fashion, music, jewellery and accessories, interspersed with numerous street food outlets. Following the passageways that lead into the old Stables the space is something closer to an alternative shopping centre rather than a market with large vintage and designer clothing outlets now occupying the converted railway arches. Further into this part of the Stables there are still a few stalls offering second-hand and collectable gear, but these are few and far between.

The Stables Market is now a large, modern shopping piazza with an internet café, food court, music store and several large retro clothing outlets. This is the second stage of a process that began with the transformation of the area between Camden Lock and the railway arches.

The hordes of teenagers that pack the stables every weekend enjoy looking for new clothing, alternative music, jewellery and accessories without any concern for what has disappeared. Amid all the African carvings, original textiles, ethnic clothing and household goods, there are a few second-hand stalls that are a throwback to the market's origins.

In the main Stables Yard there is another food court and a few new food outlets, but within the arches there are also some great vintage outlets including one called *A Dandy in Aspic* where the elegantly dressed Casper offers an incredible choice of vintage men's fashion. Next door is *The Arc* which is an equal treasure trove for female vintage fashionistas.

By the statue to Amy Winehouse there are further steps taking you into a further subterranean shopping area where you will find the very charming *Basement Tea Rooms* which is a great place to enjoy a more relaxed dining experience and is next door to Camden's largest second-hand book store with lots of cheap paperbacks to sift through. It's these hidden little areas that represent the real spirit of Camden, let's hope they survive the next wave of development.

Camden Passage

Opposite Islington Green at the junction of Upper Street
and Essex Road, N1 8EA

www.camdenpassageislington.co.uk

Twitter: @CamdenPassageN1

Tube: Angel (Northern)

Open: Wednesday, Saturday and Sunday 7am-3pm (antiques
market); Thursday 8.30am-6pm (book market)

Camden Passage is not anywhere near Camden, but lies in a
quaint pedestrian passage that runs behind Islington High
Street. The modest shop fronts, partly occupied by antique
dealers, and the flagstone paving give an old-world atmosphere
and the antiques market and the book market on Thursday add
to this sense of antiquity. The architecture is a genuine mix of
Georgian, Victorian and Edwardian, but the market and antique
dealers are far more recent, arriving in the 1960s – when Islington

began the process of gentrification that has transformed it into one of London's most desirable neighbourhoods.

The antiques market on Wednesdays, Saturdays and Sundays is a lot of fun with experienced antique dealers selling genuine antiques and objets d'art, alongside more second-hand vintage stalls. The mix is an appealing one with lots of junk to sift through for just a few quid as well as some fine antiques sold for several hundred pounds.

It is in the middle section of the market, just before the Camden Head pub, that some of the best stalls tend to congregate with enough second-hand clothes, junk and bric-à-brac to keep bargain hunters occupied for a while. Those with more money to spend and an interest in fine antiques should concentrate on the far end of the market. Here you'll find Pierrepont Arcade – a covered area with al fresco stalls and an indoor maze of units selling smaller collectables like stamps and military medals. It's around here you can also find some great things for the home such as crystal champagne glasses for not much more than the clunking supermarket alternative.

The book market on Thursdays has a completely different feel. While the antique market sells mostly upmarket items to tourists and well-to-do antique hunters, the book market is far more egalitarian. Hardbacks sell for £4 and paperbacks go for a £1 or less. Don't expect decorative antiquarian tomes, but rather popular paperbacks as well as reference books on travel, art, cooking and history.

Eat & Drink

The Camden Head is a stylish pub which is a great place for a pint. There are lots of cafés on Camden Passage, but one of the best is *Sushi Show* at number 28, offering freshly prepared sushi at a reasonable price.

Chalton Street

Chalton Street, between Euston Road and Churchway, NW1 1JD
Tube: Euston, King's Cross (Northern)
Rail: Euston, King's Cross, St Pancrass
Open: Wednesday-Friday 9am-4pm

Chalton Street is a strange anomaly, located just off the busy Euston Road and within a few minutes walk of the British Library, it caters for the Pakistani community from the surrounding estates of Somers Town as well as some passing custom from local office workers.

The market is at its busiest on a Friday, but even then there are only about ten pitches offering a mix of great value clothing, household goods, kitchenware and colourful fabrics sold by the metre. The stall selling bargain bedding and towels is run by one of the market's stalwarts, Lawrence, who has been trading here for over 30 years and has witnessed its decline in the face of stiff

competition from high street stores and now online shopping.
He remains stoical, 'You just keep going. I've been at it too long
to change...' and with that he's off to serve another customer.

The market remains a friendly place to visit and a genuine
slice of London life next to the high rise offices and heavy traffic
of Euston Road. On warm days it is a pleasant street with wide
pavements and enough cafés and eateries to allow you to relax
and enjoy some people watching.

Chapel Market

Between Liverpool Road and Baron Street, N1 9EX
Tube: Angel (Northern)
Open: Tuesday-Saturday 9am-6pm,
Sunday 8.30am-4pm (Farmers' Market)

There's been a market on this pedestrian street in Islington since around 1870 and although the area has been transformed into an expensive and upmarket part of London, this market remains a throwback to the old, working-class borough that has largely been forgotten.

As soon as you walk into the market from Liverpool Road you enter a very different world from that of Islington High Street, with stall holders chatting with their regular customers and a clear sense of community. It's really possible to do your entire weekly shop at Chapel Market with great fruit and veg stalls, a small deli van selling fine cheese and cold meats, fresh flowers, haberdashery and fabrics, fresh meat and fish, as well as stalls selling beds, carpets, cards and, of course, phone accessories. Another great addition to the market is the cycle stall which sells great value bike parts and accessories and offers a full service for just £30.

You don't have to spend very much time here to see that this market has an atmosphere and sense of place that is increasingly rare. Barry, the friendly fishmonger, has been trading here for over 30 years and is always busy offering advice or recommending a particularly good catch, even storing customers' produce until they've finished shopping. Fruit and veg seller John is one of the markets characters, having started here as a fresh faced kid back in 1974. In the intervening years he has lost none of his cheek. When one of his Turkish customers raves about her dish using his garlic and courgettes, he says:

'I don't like courgettes, I don't like garlic,
I won't be coming round yours for tea!'

It's this unique character that makes this one of the best market experiences to be had in the capital. Bring a big basket or trolley and fill your boots.

Eat & Drink

Chapel Market has a handful of street food stalls towards the end of the street which are worth checking out. If you fancy a pint look out for *The Alma* (number 77-78) and for traditional pie and mash there is *M. Manze* (74). *Alpino* (97) is a traditional Italian caff that does a great fry-up, while *Mercer & Co* (26) serves excellent coffee and accompanying treats.

"I don't like courgettes, I don't like garlic, I won't be coming round yours for tea!"

Church Street

Church Street from Edgware Road to Lisson Grove, NW8 8EU
Tube: Edgware Road (District, Metropolitan and Bakerloo)
Open: Tuesday-Saturday 9am-5pm

Church Street Market occupies a fairly central location, but few
people from outside the immediate area actually visit. If they do
it is usually by accident, or on the way to the more famous Alfies
Antiques Market (see page 65) which lies at the Lisson Grove end
of the street. For this reason, Church Street Market has managed
to maintain a friendly community feel, with lots of the stall-
holders taking time out to have a natter with regular customers
on quiet weekdays. On Saturdays the market greatly increases in
size with stalls extending the entire length of Church Street and
the crowds adding to the atmosphere, but offering traders little
time for a leisurely chat.

This part of the Edgware Road (just past the Marylebone fly-over) is pretty down-at-heel and many of the stalls concentrate on the cheap and cheerful rather than better quality goods. There are lots of good deals to be found with the £5 shoe stall at the Edgware Road entrance to the market always proving popular. Church Street is a good market to stock up on basic fresh fruit and veg, but there is not much of the exotic on offer. There is more choice when it comes to fish with three stalls setting up here on a Saturday offering anything from the humble cod to juicy king prawns and fresh squid. One trader sells surplus and slightly damaged biscuits, chocolates and other packaged foods. The service is gruff, but with lots of bargains he is always busy.

Although many of the clothes on offer on Church Street are cheap and tacky, there are several stalls selling interesting stuff. One displayed a wide range of designer T-shirts (probably copies) for only a tenner and another was offering M&S suits for just £50. Other items for sale include pet food and toys, household goods, children's clothes, fresh flowers, underwear, bedding and towels and several good value bag stalls.

At the junction with Salisbury Street, Church Street undergoes a subtle transformation as modern buildings give way to well preserved 19th century shop fronts, many of them dealing in fine antiques. It is at this part of the market that you'll find Alfies Antiques Market with five floors of antiques and a roof-top café (see page 65). The fly traders that once sold jewellery and bric-à-brac outside Alfies have long ago been driven from the street by the actions of Westminster Council. It is a pity, as this part of the market could do with a few second-hand stalls to add a bit of variety. The best thing at this end of the market is the excellent fabric stall selling basic material for as little as £1 a metre and there are one or two good fashion stalls on a Saturday offering fashionable seasonal ladies wear with colourful summer dresses for just a tenner.

Church Street market is one of the most interesting and vibrant local markets in London and certainly deserves to be more widely known. The market is relatively quite during the week and Saturdays are really the only day to go to see the place at its best.

Eat & Drink

Church Street Café (95) and *Cali Café* (39) are the best greasy spoons on the market. Further down the street you can find more exotic fare at the *Kurdistan Café* (59) and *Habaybna* (55) Arabic restaurant which caters for the local Middle-Eastern community. For a swift pint, look out for *The Traders Inn* located in the middle of the market (52).

Visit

Alfies Antiques Market is towards the end of the market and is worth a visit for vintage clothes, pictures, jewellery, furniture and other collectables (see page 65).

Hampstead Community Market

Hampstead Community Centre,
78 Hampstead High Street, NW3 1RE
www.hampsteadcommunitycentre.co.uk
Tube: Hampstead (Northern)
Open: Monday-Saturday 8.30am-5.30pm (food market), Saturday
10am-6pm (craft fair and food)
1st Sunday of the month is the antiques market; 2nd Sunday Book
Fair; 3rd Jean's Antiques and Crafts; 4th (and 5th if there is one)
Sunday Artisan Market

Hampstead Community Market has been trading for years and at
its heart are three permanent units which trade throughout the
week with a great butchers offering quality organic, free-range meat,
Hampstead Seafoods providing quality fresh fish, while *Jenkins and*

Son Fruit & Vegetables has a spectacular display of fresh produce, there's even a little snack bar. These permanent businesses occupy units adjacent to the Community Centre where a small and friendly craft fair takes place on Saturdays. The craft market has a delicious and great value café and several good quality deli stalls. The Sunday market changes from week to week with the artisan event offering a great mix of local crafts and the ever-popular second-hand book stall which has a regular following among Hampstead's literati.

Hoxton Street

Hoxton Street (between Falkirk Street and Nuttall Street), N1 6SH
www.hackney.gov.uk/hoxton-market
Twitter: @HoxtonStMarket
Tube/Rail: Old Street (Northern)
Open: Monday-Friday (street food and general) 10.30am-4pm,
Saturday (general) 10am-4pm

There has been a market on Hoxton Street since 1687, but several
of the old traders that used to set up near Nuttall Street have now
retired, leaving empty pitches even on a Saturday. The council
have made an effort to revive the market with adverts in the local
press, but many of the traders remain unimpressed and complain
about recent parking restrictions that have damaged the market.

Despite the negativity, there are still some great bargains to
be found on a Saturday with one of the longest established stalls
selling very cheap sheets, blanks and towels from boxes on the

street and Laurence's stall offering great value kitchen wear and household electricals. The young lads at the fruit and veg pitch are here all week and offer basic fresh produce sold by-the-bowl for just a pound.

Another old favourite is the stall offering hundreds of pairs of glasses at discount prices which is always popular with myopic locals. A good deal of the market on a Saturday is given over to street fashion with nothing fancy but plenty of good quality street wear for well below shop prices and many discount rails. Among the regulars is the large toiletries stall which offers anything from branded toothpaste to designer label aftershave at incredibly low prices and there's also a good value organic butchers with plenty of cheap cuts for those on a budget.

There are some new arrivals to Hoxton Street on a Saturday, with a great stationery stall offering all kinds of fine office knick-knacks at well below the prices of upmarket rivals. The other surprise addition to market is the second-hand furniture stall run by Joe, who has been trading here for a few years and does very well with the new arrivals to the area. The vintage clothing and homemade cake stall are also relatively new to the market and are signs that Hoxton Street and the surrounding area are gradually changing.

Hoxton Street is a bit more rough-and-ready than some of the more trendy east end markets, but it's none the worse for that and definitely worth a visit if only for the bargains and the banter.

Eat & Drink

There are lots of good cafés on Hoxton Street, but the red catering van at the Falkirk Street end of the market is an established favourite, belching smoke from a high funnel and producing delicious jerk chicken for which there are always long queues.

Inverness Street

Between Camden High Street and Arlington Road, NW1 7HJ
Tube: Camden Town (Northern Line)
Open: Daily 9am-6pm

There has been a market on Inverness Street since 1900 and
for much of that time it sold good quality food to the locals
of Camden. The last forty years have seen the area transform
into a tourist destination and this change has in recent years
subsumed Inverness Street, so that now the market is almost
entirely dedicated to tourist novelties, ethnic textiles but most
predominantly novelty T-Shirts. The T-shirts and sweat shirts
offer considerable variety with some advocating the smoking of
cannabis while others promote the latest bands or involve some
kind of lewd joke, and sweatshirts proclaiming the universities of
Oxford or Cambridge are also a firm favourite with visitors.

Probably the longest running stall is the one dedicated to football scarves and kit, taking pride of place at the front of the market. While the stalls selling university stuff tend to be partisan (either Oxford or Cambridge), the football stall appeals to supporters of every major team.

Inverness Street is probably busier today than when it was a traditional food market, but it's difficult to get excited about a Chinese stall worker selling a T-shirt made in Bangladesh to a Portuguese tourist. The idea of authenticity is a tricky one, but this market could serve as a good definition of the term 'inauthentic'.

Eat & Drink
There are lots of trendy cafés on Inverness Street among them *Made in Brasil* which serves a good cappuccino. For something a little stronger *The Good Mixer* at the far end of the street is a popular drinking hole.

KERB King's Cross

Granary Square, NC1 4AA
www.kerbfood.com
Twitter: @KERB_
Instagram: Kerbfood
Tube/Rail: King's Cross, St Pancras (Northern)
Open: Wedneday-Friday 12noon-2pm

From Wednesday to Friday the KERB team transform Granary
Square into a mini festival of street food with at least 8 traders
offering anything from Taiwanese Lunch Boxes to substantial
Portuguese steak sandwiches. The stalls are always rotating
but you can see the week's traders on their website. Whatever
the lineup, the quality of food is always high with vegan and
vegetarian options guaranteed. There's plenty of public seating
and a fountain with further tiered seats looking out over the
canal, making this a great market to sit, eat and chill on fine days.

Kilburn Square

Kilburn High Road between Brondesbury Road, NW6 6PP
Tube: Kilburn Park (Bakerloo)
Rail: Kilburn High Road
Open: Monday-Saturday 9.30-5.30pm

Kilburn Square is an ugly 1980's construction which has seen
better days. The market that takes place within a gated square
below the dilapidated flats has faced numerous threats of
redevelopment all of which have come to nothing. Despite all
the upheaval and the lack of investment, the market soldiers on,
offering an average range of cheap goods, supplementing the
functional selection on offer on the High Street. The fruit and
veg stall at the entrance of the gated market is always popular,
but nextdoor is a lock up that has recently been repossessed by
bailiffs. Let's hope something can be done to bring this little
market back to life.

CAR BOOT

MARKET

SALTERTON RD

EBURNE RD

SEVEN SISTERS RD

SALTERTON RD

MAYTON ST

HORNSEY RD

HERTSLET RD

SHOPPING CENTRE

TOLLINGTON RD

PARKHURST RD

WARLTERS RD

HOLLOWAY RD

CAMDEN RD

CALEDONIAN RD

JACKSON RD

HOLLOWAY RD

Nag's Head

South side of Seven Sisters Road at
Holloway Road junction, N7 6AG
www.nagsheadmarket.com
Tube: Holloway Road, Arsenal (Piccadilly)
Rail: Drayton Park
Open: Monday-Wednesday 7am-7pm (new and second-hand
goods market); Thursday-Saturday 7am-9pm (mixed market),
Sunday 7am-4pm (flea market and new goods)

Nestled behind the Nag's Head shopping centre with its main
entrance on bustling Seven Sisters Road, this market has been
fighting competition from the surrounding shops for years.
Nag's Head Market might seem like an afterthought to the
main shopping complex, but it began trading on the site in the
mid '70s before the shopping centre was built and could well
outlast its more recent competition. The market has survived by

opening daily throughout the week and offering different themes depending on the day with the flea markets proving very popular on Wednesdays and Sundays.

The market may change from day to day, but there are regular stalls that trade every day, selling necessities such as food, household goods, and new clothing. The excellent fruit and veg outlet, fishmongers, fabric stall and halal butchers are all popular features of the market. These permanent units are complimented by other stalls such as the egg man, who has been selling farm fresh eggs here every Friday and Saturday for over 30 years.

Wednesday is the biggest day, with its mixture of antiques and second-hand goods with particular strengths being used clothing and shoes. Women are well catered for with racks of dresses and labels varying from designer to High Street brands as well as a few vintage party dresses. There are also several stalls selling old records, vintage plates, and household accessories.

Nags Head Market is struggling on despite the competition and still seems to draw in the regulars with its unusual mix of new and second-hand shopping. Planning permission has been granted for improvements to the entrances and fabric of the market. On Saturdays and Sundays there is a car boot sale on the other side of Seven Sisters Road (see page 363), which is just a minute away and well worth a visit.

Eat & Drink
The number of little eateries within the market has greatly increased in recent years and there are now 11 different cuisines to choose from. Our favourite is the ever popular *Zen Washoku* for great-value Japanese food.

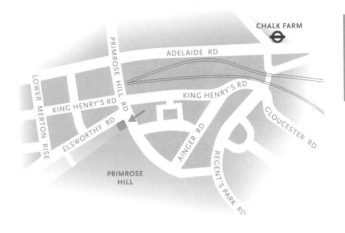

Primrose Hill Farmers' Market

St Paul's School, Primrose Hill Road, NW3 3DS
www.thespreadlondon.com
Twitter: @TheSpreadLDN
Instagram: thespreadldn
Tube: Chalk Farm (Northern)
Open: Saturday 10am-3pm

This wonderful market is run by the intrepid folk at The Spread who host several food markets across London. Every Saturday about forty stalls set out their tempting wares in a playground at the very northern tip of Primrose Hill Park. Foodie visitors to the market will not be disappointed with fresh organic fruit and veg from the likes of *Wild Country Organics* and there are even specialist tomato and mushroom traders if you're after something unusual. *Pick's Organic Farm* is always here catering for the carnivore community with a skilled butcher on hand to make sure visitors get exactly the right cut. Primrose Hill can also boast an excellent fishmonger with *Veasey & Sons* providing a spectacular display of fish and shellfish fresh from the south coast, alongside a selection of produce from their own smokehouse.

Primrose Hill is also a great place to visit for deli foods with specialist Italian, Greek, Spanish and French stalls offering anything from hand-carved Jamon Iberico to freshly made ravioli and there's also a stall offering a bewildering range of olives and stuffed peppers. For the best British produce, *Hook & Son* have delicious butter, honey and raw, organic milk, while *The Borough Cheese Company* are regulars here with a small but tempting selection of British cheeses with little tasters always on hand for the curious. There are lots of sweet things to be found at Primrose Hill, but a real favourite is the *German Wholefood Baker*, which is one of the few places in London offering genuine German cheesecake.

For those who want to eat on the go, there are several street food stalls offering anything from meatballs with pasta from *Liberty Kitchen* to mouthwatering meaty sandwiches prepared by *The Parsons Nose*.

After a visit to this vibrant market it's easy to see why the foodies of Primrose Hill have taken this place to their hearts.

BLACK
TRUFFLE OIL
PARMESAN
RICOTTA

£3.00
/tray

Queen's Crescent

Queen's Crescent, between Malden Road & Grafton Road, NW5 4HH
Tube: Chalk Farm (Northern Line)
Rail: Kentish Town West
Open: Thursday 8.30am-2.30pm (busiest day) and
Saturday 8.30am-3pm

Queen's Crescent is an anonymous street off the beaten track and
easily missed. For this reason the market that takes place here on
a Thursday and Saturday is a very local affair with people swapping
gossip as they wander from stall to stall. The area is a little run-down,
but the atmosphere is friendly, with lots of traders being on first-
name terms with their customers. Eddie has been selling great-value
kitchenware, household goods and toiletries here for over thirty years
and is always chatting with his regulars. He remembers when the
market was a lot busier and business was good, but still keeps a smile
on his face and says he's always going to trade here come rain or shine.

Queen's Crescent used to have several fruit and veg stalls, but they have now gone and the shops along the route have taken their place with stalls extending onto the pavement and lots of cheap produce to catch passing trade. The market is a good place to find really cheap street fashion with one stall selling surplus and slight seconds from M&S for a fraction of the usual price. The shoe stall is also a regular here offering basic street fashion with most shoes for around £20. Mark has been running his haberdashers stall for over twenty years and offers great value fabrics with prices starting from just £1 a metre. Like a lot of the traders at Queen's Crescent he also trades at similar markets like Hoxton and Lewisham and, like them, he is a little downhearted at the downturn in business at these traditional street markets.

This is a surprisingly easy market to get to with Kentish Town West station just five minutes walk away and this really is a great place to visit if you want a slice of genuine London life. It's a different world from the tourists and novelty tat of Camden Market and all the better for it.

Eat & Drink

There are a few good places to stop for a refuel on Queen's Crescent with *Delichio's* (number 177) being one of the most popular caffs in the area and at the other end of the market there's the *Blue Sea* (number 143) for traditional fish and chips.

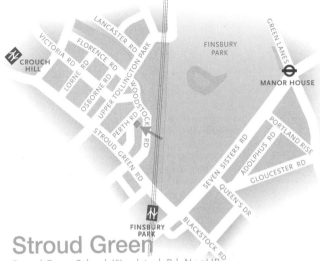

Stroud Green

Stroud Green School, Woodstock Rd, N4 3HB
www.stroudgreenmarket.com
Twitter: @StroudGrMarket
Rail: Finsbury Park, Crouch Hill
Open: Sunday 10am-2.30pm

Every Sunday the small playground of Stroud Green School is transformed into a friendly community food market offering grocery essentials including quality fruit and veg, bread and pastries, delicious cheeses, quality meat and fresh fish from the Kent coast. The market also has prepared foods, such as *Pie Station* offering all kinds of pastry delights and lots of food to eat on the go, including burgers beautifully prepared by a local chef. In addition, the market boasts a local micro brewery stall and a wine merchant offering a choice of unusual Italian wines. Stoud Green Market is run with enthusiasm by the ebullient Edmund who, along with the traders, has made this event a success.

Swiss Cottage

Eton Avenue (outside Hampstead Theatre), NW3 3EU
Tube: Swiss Cottage (Jubilee)
Rail: South Hampstead
Open: Friday & Saturday (busiest day) 9.30am-4.30pm,
Wednesday (farmers' market) 10am-4pm

Swiss Cottage market started in 1974 on undeveloped wasteland
to the north of Swiss Cottage swimming pool and library
and without the permission of Camden Council. The market
was always run on a non-profit basis by a local community
organisation. It had a friendly and rather disorganised
atmosphere with lots of interesting bookstalls, second-hand
clothing and bric-à-brac to sift through among the 50 or so
stalls. Despite the regular threats of redevelopment it remained
for many years a little oasis of community spirit amid the
commercialism and traffic of Swiss Cottage. The market was

eventually removed from its main site to make way for a new leisure complex and flats in the mid noughties.

The market is now run by Camden Council and consists of about ten stalls on the pedestrian area outside Hampstead Theatre. Continuity is provided by the redoubtable Barney, who has been selling great-value second-hand books on the market for years and recalls the days when he was joined by over forty stalls on the market's old site. The long standing stall selling New Age paraphernalia and crystals is also a throw back to this market's hippy origins. They are joined on Fridays and Saturdays by a bread stall, a few clothing traders and a couple of pitches dedicated to street food. The Wednesday farmers' market has also been going for many years and is well supported by the local community (see page 376).

Anyone who visited this market in its heyday will be sad to see what it's become, but the place is still worth visiting if you're around Swiss Cottage, particularly on fine days when the pedestrian area with its public benches can be put to good use.

Eat & Drink

The Thai food stall is one of the market's major attractions. If the weather is bad you could try the café in the Hampstead Theatre.

Visit

The Freud Museum (20 Maresfield Gardens, www.freud.org.uk) is based at Freud's last home. The library across the square from the market is well worth a look at for its period piece interior. Sporty types might be attracted by the swimming pool and new gym.

Tottenham Green

Town Hall Approach, N15 4RY
www.tottenhamgreenmarket.co.uk
Twitter: @MarketTottenham
Tube/Rail: Seven Sisters (Victoria) or Tottenham Hale
Open: Sunday 11am-4pm

This little market has a really friendly atmosphere and offers a great selection of meat, locally sourced honey, natural cosmetics, a small selection of fine wines and some great pastries and breads including from the family run *Prestige Patisserie*. If you just want to eat on the go there are a handful of street food stalls including the ironically named *Pig Out*, offering vegan fast food, the delicious dumpling seller and a great Satay stall. There is also *Craving Coffee*, offering great coffee from local suppliers. This is a wonderful little market which has engaged and is supported by the local community – long may it survive and thrive!

West

West

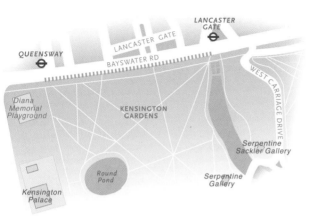

Bayswater Road
Art Exhibition

South side of Bayswater Road
from Lancaster Gate to Queensway, W2 4RQ
www.bayswater-road-artists.co.uk
Twitter: @BayswaterART
Tube: Lancaster Gate, Queensway (Central)
Open: Sunday 8am-4pm

On a fine Sunday this stretch of Bayswater Road is like an outdoor
art gallery (if you can ignore the touristy souvenir stalls), but minus
the pretension and, occasionally, without the artistry. Most of the
artists are on hand to sell their paintings, and many of them take
credit cards. This is a sophisticated market, even though its wares
are largely aimed at tourists. All styles of painting are covered from
Renaissance to Pop Art. Tourists have a wealth of schlock from
which to choose including Oxford sweatshirts, London T-shirts and

key rings and refrigerator magnets with emblems of the capital. For those on a tight budget there are mini prints with magnets on the back for just £2 each and plenty of miniature paintings depicting London for around £10.

The many animal paintings (both oil and watercolour) range from elephants and lions to hens and horses with a significant number of artists devoting themselves to dogs and cats. Cityscapes (London to New York), seascapes (with plenty of tropical beach scenes) and landscapes (from battles to Turneresque renderings) are all strongly represented. One of the busiest stalls sells pictures of famous London scenes made from clock parts with a working clock incorporated into the design – Big Ben is an obvious favourite for this unusual art form. Most of the vendors advertise in more than one language and will pack up paintings to be shipped abroad – more evidence that this market is not geared for native Londoners.

There are plenty of portrait artists here depicting Native Americans, iconic Americans like Marilyn Monroe and Woody Allen and famous Brits like David Beckham. Landscapes here tend to be restricted to either Mediterranean villages, tropical beach scenes or romantic paintings of women sleeping in groves, on balconies, under trees, etc. If you want something a little more personal there is an artist who makes personalised birth and wedding announcements and is particularly in demand for her children's name plates. There is more modern art on Bayswater Road with plenty of vibrant squares of colour and abstract paintings. Of course, there are also some weird pieces too, such as the Disney characters painted on papyrus and oil paintings of modern airline jets.

It is easy to make fun of the art on Bayswater on a Sunday, but among all the derivative stuff there are quite a few genuine artists. Walking along the pavements talking with the artists and occasionally finding something that grabs your interest is a great way to spend a couple of hours on a Sunday and who knows, you may come away with something for your wall.

Eat & Drink

Lo Spuntino is a popular café on the junction with Queensway. If you fancy a pint *The Swan* is at 66 Bayswater Road and has outdoor seating for when the weather is fine.

Visit

Hyde Park has lots to offer on fine days including boating on the Serpentine or a visit to The Serpentine Gallery. On Sunday there is always the appeal of Speakers Corner, where members of the public are encouraged to get on their soap box and put the world to rights.

Duck Pond Market
Richmond

Heron Square, Richmond upon Thames, TW9 1EP
www.duckpondmarket.com
Twitter: @duckpondmarket
Instagram: @duckpondmarket
Tube/Rail: Richmond (District)
Parking at Whittaker Avenue Car Park
Saturday 11am-4pm (Foodies), Sunday 10.30am-5pm (Artisan)
The good folk at Duck Pond run a number of markets across
London with their flagship event being in Ruislip (see page 131).
The weekend market in Richmond is a much smaller affair with
about 30-40 stalls on a Sunday and around 20-25 every Saturday.
Saturday is designated as a foodie market and artisans are to the
fore on a Sunday, but in reality there's a good mix of food and
artisan products on both days.

Sheltered within this charming square you can find a number of jewellers selling their own designs, colourful handmade purses, a local artist selling photographic images and a company offering all kinds of lamps and jewellery made from recycled scientific equipment and watch parts, including cufflinks made from old typewriter keys. One textile artist makes handmade fabric creations from masks to soft toys, cushions to bunting. Another interesting stall specialises in vintage and collectable jewellery and tableware with anything from an antique hat pin to a sterling silver gravy boat. For those looking to treat a furry friend, there's also a pet stall with lots of dog-and cat-themed gifts and fancy pet foods. At the entrance to the market, don't miss the display of *Timshel Design* wooden chairs which are beautiful, hand-made and are priced accordingly. Each week the mix of traders is slightly different, but the one thing they all have in common is that they offer products that are ethically and sustainably made.

Food is always on the menu here with a great choice of street food including Mexican and Colombian delicacies and lots of pies, pastries, brownies, cakes and breads to eat on the go or take away to enjoy at home. The *Aroma Organic* selection of sausage rolls and pies are particularly appetising and if meat is your thing there is always *Griddly Greens* that offers free range sausage or bacon sandwiches and burgers.

Heron Square is a prefect location for the market with enough places to sit and relax with your food. The market might not have a duck or a pond, but if you walk through the opposite arch you can get a great view of the Thames flowing past.

Duck Pond Market Ruislip

The Great Barn, Manor Farm, Ruislip, HA4 7QL
www.duckpondmarket.com
Twitter: @duckpondmarket
Instagram: @duckpondmarket
Tube: Ruislip (Metropolitan or Piccadilly), West Ruislip (Central)
Rail: West Ruislip
Free parking St Martin's Approach car park
Open: First Sunday 10am-3pm (Foodies),
Third Sunday 10am-3pm (Artisan)
Duck Pond Markets run great food and artisan events in various
locations across London with a commitment to local products,
ethically and sustainably made. Their fortnightly market in
Ruislip could be considered their flagship, with as many as 100
traders setting up within a quaint 13th century converted barn
and courtyard. The eponymous duck pond is also just a stone's

throw away. West Ruislip is the last stop on the Central Line, but it's a charming little place and really does feel like a million miles from London, making it a great way to escape the capital without going to too much trouble.

On any market day you can expect to find a great selection of jewellery, clothing, household textiles, artwork, kids' toys, natural cosmetics and perfume and even a used vinyl stall. One advantage of travelling this far out is that the prices are lower than more central markets with some really good deals, including natural kingsize quilts for just £95 and a great up-cycled chest of drawers for only £80.

Even on the third Sunday, dedicated to arts and crafts, there's a good deal of quality food and wine here with several street food stalls in the courtyard offering anything from fresh pizza to organic burgers.

The Duck Pond people make a real effort to ensure this event is a lot of fun with face painting, hair plaiting and a petting zoo for restless kids and massages for their stressed parents as well as regular live music to accompany the experience.

North End Road

East side of North End Rd,
from Walham Grove to Lillie Rd, SW6 1NW
www.lbhf.gov.uk/ner
Twitter: @NorthEndRdMrkt
Tube: Fulham Broadway (District)
Open: Monday-Saturday 7am-5pm (Saturday busiest day)
The area north of Fulham Broadway is a real social and cultural
mix and North End Road Market reflects this diversity with
shoppers from the smart Victorian terraces rubbing shoulders
with those from the local estates as they all go about their grocery
shopping. The market is still a busy and vibrant place to shop
with quality fishmongers and a stall specialising in farm fresh
eggs – including huge goose eggs which you won't find at any
supermarket. There are no meat stalls here, but there are several
quality butchers along the street which supplement the activity
on the market.

The fruit and veg stalls are the most prominent feature of North End Road with lots of competition among the traders. Some of the best stalls still make the effort with old-fashioned displays of regimented pears and apples sitting pertly on pink tissue paper. Geoffrey's fruit and veg pitch is at the north end of the market and is one of the most popular. The stall has been in the family for several generations and Geoffrey continues to trade here six days a week, just like his father and grandfather. Becky's flower stall is a much-loved feature of the market and Becky has become as well known as her dad, Cyril, who started the business over 70 years ago.

The French cheese van has been trading here for years and on Saturdays is joined by several other foodie traders including the Greek olive stall and one specialising in Ethiopian coffee. There are still a few clothing stalls on the market including a great value seller of scarves and pashminas and Kirsty's stall specialising in quality kids' shoes and clothing. A few of the household goods stalls have left the market in recent years and are now replaced by street food stalls offering anything from falafel to Indian curry.

The market might not be worth going out of your way to visit for these simple groceries, but on four days a year the North End Road is transformed into a major festival when the street is pedestrianised and a whole host of additional gift stalls, live music and events make the market a major attraction. For more information about the seasonal markets take a look at their website and Twitter feed.

Eat & Drink

At the centre of the market is *Jaffa Bake House* which is known
for it's delicious Palestinian flatbreads and a little further north is
The Goose public house. At the very southern end of the market
is the pedestrianised Jerdan Place with several cafés and plenty of
outdoor seating.

Visit

For second-hand bargain shopping there are quite a few charity
shops along North End Road. On Wednesdays, Fridays and
Saturdays there is a popular tabletop sale at St John's Churchyard at
the southern end of the market which is worth checking out for its
mix of bric-à-brac, vintage clothing and accessories.

West

Partridges
Food Market

Duke of York Square, Chelsea, SW3 4LY

www.partridges.co.uk

Twitter: @partridgesfoods

Tube: Sloane Square (Circle and District)

Open: Saturday 10am-4pm

Started by the eponymous grocery store in 2005 with just 15 stalls, Partridges Food Market has gone from strength to strength and now has 70 quality food stalls setting up in this smart Chelsea square every Saturday. The market offers a great mix of freshly-prepared food which can be cooked at home or street food to eat on the go. For grocery shopping there are some excellent butchers, a seasonal fruit and veg stall along with delicious breads, prepared meats, olives and deli dishes, fresh pasta as well as cakes and cheeses. If you can't find all that you need there is always *Partridges* itself, just next to the market.

The street food here is incredibly varied with fresh oysters for a pound each making a great starter to your journey through the market. Among the treats here are delicious fish burgers, substantial Greek wraps and sushi which you can see being prepared, as well as substantial organic burgers cooked by the butchers who supply the meat.

The energy of this market is really infectious and the foodies here are always willing to dispense advice, cooking suggestions or simply talk about the provenance of their produce. There are a few places to sit and enjoy your food, but most people choose to amble among the stalls while enjoying the dish of their choice.

Visit

Just behind the market is the Saatchi Gallery which is dedicated to modern art and has a busy programme of exhibitions which are always worth exploring.

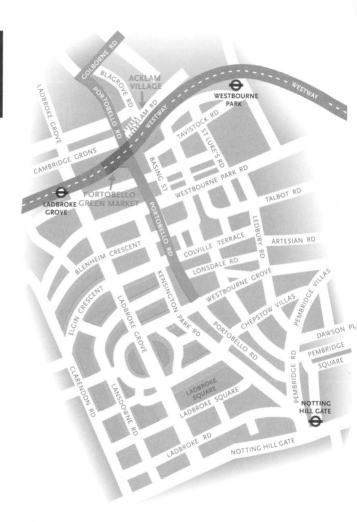

Portobello

Portobello Road from (and including) Golborne Road to
Chepstow Villas, W10 5TE
www.portobelloroad.co.uk
Tube: Notting Hill Gate (Central, Circle or District), Ladbroke
Grove (Hammersmith & City)
Open: Monday-Wednesday, Friday-Saturday 8am-6.30pm,
Thursday 8am-1pm (general market);
Friday 8am-5pm, Saturday 6am-5.30pm (Antiques), Friday-Sunday
8am-5.30pm (Portobello Green – under Westway), Monday-
Saturday 9am-5pm (Golborne Road)

"the best and oddest market for antiques in London." V.S. Pritchett

Shopping is possible on Portobello Road all week, but the market
is famous for its Saturday antiques market. Antiques have been
sold here since the 18th century and the tradition is still going
strong with over 400 antique dealers showing up on a Saturday and
tens of thousands of tourists joining the noisy procession along
the road. On a busy Saturday it is possible to walk one hundred
meters and hear languages from around the world – many of them
spoken by people who live in the area, because Portobello is home
to several immigrant communities who have added a little of their
own flavour to the mix of food, clothing, bric-à-brac and antiques
that make up this unique area of London.

   The southern end of the market definitely caters to a more
affluent crowd with its genuine antiques and as you head north,
the goods become more modern, less posh and, perhaps, more
interesting. If you're looking for the next big fashion trend, the
northern end is a good place to start as many young designers
hawk their creative wares under the vast white canopy that forms
part of what is called Portobello Green Market.

Portobello Market extends for well over a mile on a Saturday and the review for the market is divided into six sections to give a detailed account of how the market transforms itself from vast antiques market in the south to a small collection of food and bric-à-brac stalls at the northern end on Golborne Road. If you want the whole Portobello experience then Saturday is the only day to visit, when all parts of the market are going at full tilt. If you want to avoid the crowds then Friday can also be a lot of fun and the vintage market at Portobello Green is well worth exploring. Even the flea market under the Westway can be a great way to spend a relaxing Sunday morning when the rest of the market is closed. If you like food shopping then the weekday market which takes place between Lonsdale and Lancaster Road is a great place to find quality produce with particularly good fruit and veg. Portobello is one of London's most famous markets and continues to be one of the best.

Chepstow Villas to Lonsdale Road
(antiques and collectables)
This is the first part of Portobello Market when approaching from Notting Hill tube station, but the place is quiet throughout the week with just a handful of antique stalls showing up on a Friday. It is on Saturdays that the area from Chepstow Villas to Lonsdale Road is transformed into London's largest antiques market with over 100 stalls trading on the pavement and many more from the numerous indoor markets that lie along this stretch of quaint 19th century shop fronts. There are all manner of antiques and collectables to be found here, from rare and expensive items of silverware and crystal, to more quirky stalls selling cheap bric-à-brac for just a few pounds. Lonsdale Road is basically the finishing point for the antiques traders even though a few stragglers can be found beyond this point.

Lonsdale Road to Lancaster Road
(Food, flowers and clothing)

The antiques market peters out at the junction with Lonsdale Road and is replaced by an assortment of food and new fashion stalls. While the clothing is reasonable quality street fashion the real appeal of this part of Portobello is the excellent food. There are all kinds of fruit and veg to be found here from basics to more exotic produce catering for the varied cultural mix of the area with yams and cassava displayed alongside fresh limes and coriander. The stalls vary in style from the elaborate to the more mundane, but the quality and freshness of the produce is consistently high. Accompanying the fruit and veg is a long established *G. Piper & Son* fresh fish stall, a good value butchers, several deli stalls offering fine cheeses and prepared meats and a choice of stalls offering fresh baked breads, pastries and cakes.

Eat & Drink
If you're feeling peckish there are lots of street food stalls on the market including the German Sausage stall which has been here for years and can easily be found by following the delicious smell. *Books for Cooks* at 4 Blenheim Crescent is the only specialist cookbook shop in London and has a wonderful café at the back. *The Coffee Plant* at 180 Portobello Road is a specialist coffee store and a great place to get a caffeine fix.

Lancaster Road to the Railway Bridge
(New Clothing and household goods)
Here the market concentrates on the kind of new clothes and household goods to be found at most local markets. The goods are not very inspirational but there are enough good quality designer copies to make the area worth a gander. Handbags, watches, fabric, scarves and trainers are all up for grabs along this stretch of the market. Occasionally, you might just find something of interest amid the dross. The haberdashery stall is here on Fridays and Saturdays and has been in the family and on the market for over 50 years and always has a colourful display of their wares.

Portobello Green Market
Under the Westway and west up to Ladbroke Grove
(Retro and new clothing, vinyl, books and collectables)
www.portobellofashionmarket.com
Instagram: @portobellogreenmarket
Twitter: @Portobello6
Friday 10am-5pm (Vintage), Saturday 9am-5pm (Fashion),
Sunday 10am-4pm (Flea Market)
The first railway bridge marks the beginning of a funkier and more entertaining part of Portobello with the emphasis on vintage and second-hand clothing and bric-à-brac. Under the roaring Westway flyover, with its own canopied roof, you will find Portobello Green Market, which is one of the best places for vintage and second-hand fashion from Friday to Sunday. Fridays have acquired a particular reputation for lovers of vintage threads and you can often find some of the specialist fashion sellers that exhibit at the more exclusive vintage fairs also selling their wares here, with perhaps more room to barter at this cheaper open air market. Fridays and Sundays are great days to visit if you just want to indulge in vintage fashion, but to get the full Portobello experience you'll need to come on a Saturday when the whole of Portobello is alive and kicking.

Acklam Village
Just opposite Portobello Green Market and Cambridge Gardens
Friday 10am-5pm, Saturday 9am-5pm
This area of Portobello, running parallel to the Westway flyover, used to be a place for second-hand and vintage wares, but over the years has been transformed into a dedicated street food market with over 50 stalls offering food from around the world in a crowded environment closer to a music festival than a conventional market. Expect funky music, colourful characters and delicious food.

Portobello Road from Acklam Road to Golborne Road
(Retro and new clothing, bric-à-brac,furniture and electrical goods)
Friday 9am-5pm, Saturday 9am-5pm
This final stretch of Portobello Road leading up to Golborne Road is largely dedicated to second-hand clothing and bric-à-brac. There are lots of bargains to be found here including one trader who sells an assortment of second-hand clothing for just £1 a garment and plenty of great bric-à-brac stalls offering anything from religious iconography to small items of furniture with plenty of boxes of junk to sift through for the occasional gem. Scattered among the second-hand traders are several dealers in quality designer ware with one trader specialising in fine, hand-made pottery and wooden spoons. Further up, the store *Sir Plus*, has an elaborate set of high tech stalls displaying their range of stylish menswear while *Moroccan White* are regulars here with a selection of fine carpets and housewares.

Golborne Road Market
(Junk, furniture, fruit and veg and plants)
Running from Portobello Road to St Ervans Road, Golborne Road market is at the heart of Moroccan and Portuguese London. The area is still a little rough around the edges but there are signs of gentrification with several antique shops now established here. This a great place to escape the tourists while enjoying a bit of the Portobello Road experience. On weekdays it is a local market selling fruit and veg and household goods, but on Fridays and Saturdays there are lots of traders who deal in bric-à-brac and second-hand goods with a sea of junk extending onto the pavement on fine days. Holly and Nikki's plant stall, at the far end of the market, is always popular with its great range of healthy looking plants for the home and garden.

Drink
One of the best places to relax after the long trawl along Portobello Road is *Lisboa Patisserie* (57 Goldbourne Road) which serves delicious Portuguese pastries and strong coffee.

Visit
Architectural enthusiasts should look out for the soaring Trellick Tower that can be seen in the distance. It was designed by Erno Goldfinger in the late '60s and is now a Grade-II listed building. There are several great vintage stores on Golborne Road including *Doll House* (at number 90) and *Emma Goldman* (at number 112).

Shepherd's Bush

Between Uxbridge Road and Goldhawk Road W12
www.myshepherdsbushmarket.com
Twitter: @MyShepherdsBush
Tube: Shepherd's Bush Market, Goldhawk Road (Circle,
Hammersmith & City)
Open: Monday-Saturday 9am-6pm

For over a hundred years there were two tube stations bearing the
name Shepherd's Bush, but in 2008 the station on the Circle and
Hammersmith & City line became known as Shepherd's Bush
Market. This makes the market that trades along the pedestrian
thoroughfare and lock-ups between Uxbridge and Goldhawk Road,
the only one in the capital to have a tube station named after it.
The distinction must seem a little hollow as the traders have been
fighting development plans which has seen a compulsory purchase
order overturned and plans for redevelopment put on hold.

Entering from Goldhawk Road, it's clear that this place embodies the diversity of the community with many African, Middle-Eastern, West Indian and Asian locals shopping and trading from a variety of shops, lock-ups and stalls all vying for your attention as they extend parallel to the tube line with only the occasional sight of a train rumbling overhead, and the weather, to remind you that this is still London and not some foreign bazaar.

The market is not just one avenue, but also has a fairly large square on the western side of the line which is connected via two narrow arches. It is in this smaller maze of shops that most of the specialist African food stalls can be found, along with the usual mix of street fashion, cheap shoes, bags and a few outlets selling fabric by the metre. Anthony has been selling great value menswear here since flares were in fashion and depends on visitors from the Middle-East who are his main customers.

The market is especially strong on fresh food, with many top-notch fruit and veg stalls including *Fletcher's* on the corner of Goldhawk Road where Silvee has been working for over 55 years – and now has a smile on her face following the market's reprieve from redevelopment. There are also several good butchers within the market selling basics as well as more recherché things to cater for the African community such as pigs trotters and cows' tongues. Likewise, there are plenty of good fresh fish stalls offering anything from smoked haddock to fresh tuna and red snapper.

Shepherd's Bush Market is something of a throwback to an earlier time, particularly compared to the nearby Westfield Shopping Centre that now dominates the shopping environment around Shepherd's Bush Green. There are plans for a new market space on what is called the Old Laundry Site but at the moment building work is still in progress. Let's hope the future plans allow this unique market and its traders the chance to survive and thrive.

Eat & Drink

There are several good falafel stalls and Middle-Eastern cafés within the market and carnivores should look out for the *Woody Grill* (1 Uxbridge Road) which is popular with the locals.

Visit

The Bush Theatre is located at the Uxbridge Road end of the market, offering lots of theatrical shows as well as a popular café.

Southwest

Brixton

Brixton Station Road, Pope's Road, Atlantic Road,
Electric Road and Electric Avenue, SW9 8PD
www.brixtonmarket.net
Twitter: @_brixtonmarket
Tube/Rail: Brixton (Victoria Line)
Open: Monday-Saturday 8am-5.30pm, Wednesday 8am-1pm

Brixton was a smart place one hundred years ago and there are
still signs of its Edwardian grandeur in some of the architecture,
particularly along Electric Avenue (which was one of the first
streets to have electricity in the 1870's). The area was in decline
for many years but took on a new lease of life when West Indians
settled here after the war and Brixton Market adapted to cater
for the newcomers with lots of stalls offering exotic fabrics and
unusual ingredients joining the usual array of household goods
and everyday fruit and veg.

Today Brixton remains not one market, but a complicated mix of street trading, Edwardian shopping arcades and even a new shopping and eating area (Pop Brixton) constructed from shipping containers which also runs its own occasional markets. Brixton has been given a new lease of life in the last ten years as the two largest arcades have had a revamp and many of the units that were once empty are now occupied with smart eateries and gift shops. The mix of old traders and new arrivals is part of what makes Brixton a great place to explore amid its sprawling mix of roads, arcades and railway arches. The experience can be a bit disorientating, but there are plenty of watering holes for those who need to stop and get their bearings.

Brixton Station Road

This part of Brixton used to be renowned for the number and diversity of its second-hand stalls and shops trading from the railway arches. A lot of this stuff has now gone but on the corner of Brixton Road there are a handful of stalls selling bedding, African textiles, street food and one lone second-hand stall which offers a great selection of bric-à-brac and is always busy. Nev and his hat stall are also regulars here offering a selection of cool caps and sharp hats at reasonable prices. Close to the junction with Pope's Road is the last remaining railway arch dedicated to second-hand clothing, which is well worth a visit.

Pop Brixton

Junction of Brixton Station Road and Pope's Road
www.popbrixton.org
This complex of shipping containers has provided a home for lots of Brixton's independent businesses offering great street food, regular mini-market events and the wonderful *Make Do and Mend* selling vintage clothes at reasonable prices with always a few discounted rails for the hard-core bargain hunter. Pop Brixton is particularly good in the summer months with plenty of outdoor seating.

Pope's Road

This road leads on from Electric Avenue, but has none of its charm. In place of grand architecture there's a railway bridge and a vast brick wall which is usually the site of some impressive street art. In terms of the market there are quite a few quality fruit and veg stalls as well as cheap fashion and shoes, kids' clothing, small electrical goods, kitchenware and one stall specialising in cheap plastic toys. Look out for one of the longest running stalls belonging to the ever friendly Stefan, who has been selling great-value bedding and towels on Pope's Road for over 30 years. One of the entrances to Brixton Village is on Pope's Road.

Electric Avenue

This is one of the main thoroughfares of the market and a great place to start if your interest is food shopping. There are lots of excellent fruit and veg stalls here, as well as several top-notch fishmongers and butchers to complement the market. Near the junction with Atlantic Road there's a very good Thai supermarket emphasising Brixton's cultural and culinary diversity. Food isn't the only thing on offer here and there are a number of stalls selling consumer durables like street fashion, jewellery, bedding and towels, fabric by the metre, household goods, bags, accessories and watches. It's worth raising your eyes from the market to take notice of the rather grand architecture that curves above the functional shop fronts, giving some clue to Brixton's past prosperity.

Brixton Village

The largest arcade in Brixton Market has experienced something of a transformation in recent years with the traditional traders who offer delicious fresh meat, fish and vegetables being joined by a whole host of new more upmarket businesses. The new arrivals include *Champagne + Fromage*, *Honest Burgers* and some very interesting gift shops such as *Circus* and the wonderful *Brixton Cornercopia*. It would be easy to dismiss all this activity as gentrification, but these avenues were unoccupied a decade ago and now they are busy, while the traditional traders are still largely here and hopefully benefiting from the passing trade.

Market Row

This indoor arcade between Atlantic Road and Electric Lane has high ceilings and plenty of natural light making it a pleasant place to shop. A recent revamp has given the place a new lease of life with some reliably good eateries like *Pieminister* and *Franco Manca* offering great food and smarter independent shops (including *Ismad London* for expensive leather bags and *Vintage Planet*) catering to the new clientele with more money to spend. These relatively new arrivals sit alongside some real old-school retailers including some great fishmongers, butchers and several greengrocers catering for the local West Indian community.

Reliance Arcade

This narrow passageway is darker than the other arcades in the market and has only a handful of stalls offering kids' clothes and Christian iconography as well as being home to an excellent music outlets selling CDs and vinyl.

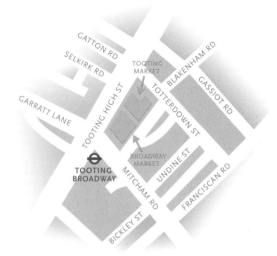

Broadway & Tooting Markets

Broadway

29 Tooting High Street, SW17 0RJ
www.broadwaymarkettooting.co.uk
Twitter/Instagram: @bwmarkettooting
Tube: Tooting Broadway (Northern)
Open: Monday-Saturday 9.30am-5pm, Wednesday until 1pm

Broadway Market doesn't look like much from the outside with its narrow entrance on Tooting High Street, crammed between rundown shop fronts, but there are some pleasant surprises to be found inside. Broadway still has its traditional mix of cheap household goods, Afro-Caribbean and Asian foods and clothing, butchers, a great value fishmongers and a pet stall complete with noisy budgies looking for a new home. The excellent fruit and veg stall at the back of the market is also a firm favourite. These traditional traders have been joined by a host of new and trendy eateries including *Hinata Japanese Food Bar*, *Hometown Rolls and Baguettes* and the ultra trendy *Pedal Back Café* that serves great coffee and is as a social hub for many of Tooting's cycling community. Even the old fishmongers now looks across at a fancy eatery – the *Sea Garden & Grill*. The traditional butchers now has *L'Amuse-Bouche* as a neighbour, but the new and the old seem to rub along well together and it's great to see this old arcade now busy again.

Tooting

21-23 Tooting High Street, SW17 0SN
www.tootingmarket.com
Twitter: @TootingMarket
Tube: Tooting Broadway (Northern)
Open: Monday-Thursday 8am-6pm,
Friday-Saturday 8am-10.30pm, Sunday 9am-5pm
Tooting Market still has its traditional fruit and veg stall on the High Street selling cheap veggie basics by the bowl, but beyond the old exterior this market has undergone a real transformation. At the centre of the L-shaped avenue, *Brickwood* coffee bar has a large illuminated sign saying TOOTING - SO COOL RIGHT NOW, and this really sums up what's been happening here. Tooting Market now has a vinyl specialist, lots of trendy bars and eateries including *Koi Ramen* and a branch of *Franco Manca* plus a host of small, well-decorated gift shops and there is even a trendy gentlemen's barbers at the back of the market. There are still a few pockets of the old Tooting, with the traditional butchers and Portuguese café still doing well and it's great to see that the market thriving when back in the 1990's it looked on its last legs.

Hildreth Street

Hildreth Street, SW12 9RQ
Tube: Balham (Northern)
Rail: Balham
Open: Monday-Saturday 9.30am-5pm, Wednesdays until 1pm

Hildreth Street market has been running in this pedestrianised corridor between grand Toblerone-roofed Victorian buildings for over one hundred years. The area has changed a good deal since those early days and the street is now full of trendy eateries and independent shops. The two regular stalls on the market offer great fruit and veg and a good range of cut flowers and potted plants. These stalwarts are joined on Saturdays by a women's clothing stall and the very excellent *London Cheese Mongers*, who have built up a loyal following among the cheese eating surrender monkeys of Balham. The market might be small, but it is loved and cherished by the locals, and long may it continue.

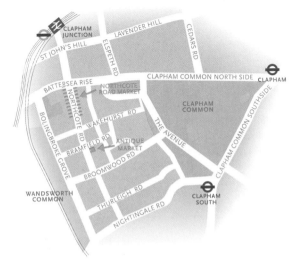

Northcote Road

North end of Northcote Road, SW11 1PA

www.northcoteroad.london/market/

Tube: Clapham Common, Clapham South (Northern)

Rail: Clapham Junction

Open: Monday-Saturday 9am-5pm,

Wednesday 9am-1pm (busiest on Saturdays)

Northcote Road has changed a great deal over the years and is now a smart shopping street with boutiques, coffee shops and delis lining the route and catering for the more prosperous locals who have brought a wave of gentrification to the area. The market has survived by smartening up their old barrows with a lick of paint and in some cases making their street stalls into almost permanent units, as well as selling merchandise that appeal to this new clientele.

There are four traders that have been here for years and form the backbone of the market. The first of these is *The Flower Stand*

Battersea which occupies a large permanent pitch on the junction with Cairns Road and always has a luscious display of cut flowers and bedding plants. The fishmongers once had a shop on the street but have now decamped to a mobile unit on the corner of Shelgate Road, where they have continued to thrive, offering a great selection of fresh fish and shellfish and a filleting service, if you need your scaly purchases prepared for table. Further down, just next to Mallinson Road, is the fabulous *Breadstall*, selling freshly made breads and pastries and offering delicious pizzas, pies and sandwiches to eat on the go. There is only one regular fruit and veg stall on the market these days, but they have been here for years and still trade from the old barrows that have been in the family for generations, although the traders of the past would probably be a bit baffled by the artichokes, asparagus, celeriac and oyster mushrooms which are now regularly on display here.

These four established traders work throughout the week, but from Friday to Sunday they are joined by a newer crowd offering great value designer women's wear, *Jenny Betts Soy Candles*, a few street food stands, *Laura Amos'* sweet desserts, the colourful olive stall and a regular here selling quality baby tops for just a tenner.

Northcote Road is a special market with a long history and although they don't have everything you could want from a market, there is a a good butchers (*Hennessy's*) and a quality cheesemonger in *Hamish Johnston* which add to appeal of the place. The street also puts on occasional events in the summer and around Christmas, when the street is pedestrianised and a lot more arts and crafts and gift stalls join the regulars.

Eat & Drink

There are lots of eateries along Northcote Road including *Brew* at number 45, the always busy *Bill's Dinner* at 54 and *Café Tamra* a little further along at number 63.

Northcote Road Antiques Market

155a Northcote Road, SW11 6QB

www.northcoateroadantiques.co.uk

Twitter: @NorthcoteRd

Rail: Clapham Junction, Clapham South (Northern)

Open: Monday-Saturday 10am-5.30pm, Sunday 12noon-5pm

Just a five minute walk south from Northcote Road Market is this inconspicuous little shop front. Appearances can be deceptive, and beyond the narrow entrance the space opens out, Tardis like, to reveal two floors and a central atrium complete with a glass roof that allows light into the further recesses. This quaint antiques centre is home to 30 dealers offering all kinds of antiques and collectables from furniture and framed pictures to household goods. The place is a real treasure trove and well worth seeking out if you're in the area.

Putney Market

St Mary's Church Square, 5 Putney High Street, SW15 1RB
www.putneymarket.com
Twitter/Instagram: @putneymarket
Tube: East Putney, Putney Bridge (District); Rail: Putney
Open: Saturday 10am-3pm

This local food market is relatively small with about 10-15 stalls, but it packs quite a culinary punch with enough quality traders to do a week's shopping if you need. Here you can find fresh fish and excellent organic meat, artisan breads and pastries and fine cheeses from the *Borough Cheese Company*. There are also a few stalls offering an excellent selection of seasonal fruit and veg.

If all the fresh produce has made you peckish there are a few caterers here offering anything from freshly made pizza to spicy Colombian street food. The church square is a great place to relax on fine days, with plenty of seating and shade provided by mature trees.

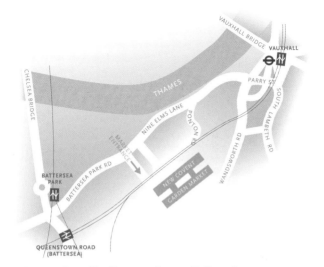

Vauxhall Sunday Market

Nine Elms Lane, SW8 5AL
www.saundersmarkets.co.uk
Tube/Rail: Vauxhall (Victoria)
Rail: Battersea Park, Queenstown Road
Open: Sunday 7am-2pm

Vauxhall Market has changed a lot in recent years and is bigger
and more popular than ever – there are now signs for the market
in Vauxhall tube station, giving some indication of just how
important it is to the area. The signs are usually not needed –
just follow the crowds heading in the direction of the market on
any Sunday. The social make up of the area and those coming
to the market has also changed with many of London's Eastern
European and African communities visiting and trading here.
You can hear anything from Russian to Yoruba spoken, amid the
cockney, as you make you make your way towards the event.

The market takes place in the concrete landscape and steel warehousing of New Covent Garden wholesale market and the Sunday market is managed by *Saunders Markets* on behalf of the New Covent Garden Market Authority. The site might lack the charm of places like Portobello and Brick Lane, but it does have an atmosphere all of its own, complete with loud music, the smell of freshly cooked foods and the sounds of thousands of people chatting and joking as they wonder the aisles in search of a bargain.

Clothing is a big feature of the market with several stalls offering piles of boxer shorts, T-shirts, ladies' underwear and socks at incredibly low prices. It's worth looking around before you part with your cash, because further into the market there are stalls offering high-quality High Street returns and surplus stock for a fraction of the the usual price, and nearly all the garments sell for between five and ten pounds. There are also great shoe stalls offering anything from workaday boots to designer trainers, but all at well below shop prices. Kitchenware, bedding, toys, plants, DIY tools and materials, towels and bedding are all to be found here with the one common denominator being very low prices. Ironically, although New Covent Garden is one of the country's largest fruit and veg wholesale markets there is only a limited range of veg on a Sunday. What is available is good value with lots of fruit and veg sold by the box or large bag for just a few quid.

Running parallel to the market is a large car boot sale run by the same organisers. The far end of the concrete complex is the heart of the car boot. Here you can find lots of second-hand gear including bikes, tools, clothing and all kinds of car boot clobber from a china Alsatian to a well used industrial drill. Visitors will find it hard to tell where the market ends and the car boot sale begins, but in truth the market and car boot combine to make one event with a great mix of new and used goods.

Eat & Drink

This kind of market has its fare share of stalls offering burgers and fry-ups, but the diversity of the visitors is reflected in the food available. Here you can find freshly made paella, Middle-Eastern delicacies as well as great value curries. All the food stalls provide seating so you can relax, enjoy your meal and do a bit of people watching.

Visit

Battersea Park is one of London's largest and grandest parks and is just ten minutes walk from the market. If you fancy a bit of Sunday culture, Tate Britain is just one tube stop away in Pimlico.

Venn Street

Venn Street, Clapham, SW4 0AT
www.vennstreetmarket.co.uk
Twitter: @vennstmarket
Tube: Clapham Common (Northern)
Open: Saturday 10am-4pm

Venn Street Market started in 2009 and is one of the good news stories on the London market scene. Every Saturday the market brings together around forty-five quality food suppliers, street food traders and the occasional handmade craft stall – all crammed into this narrow avenue which in recent years has been pedestrianised.

Just a few minutes stroll from Clapham Common, Venn Street is well worth making a journey to visit with great cheese from the likes of *Borough Cheese Co*, a choice of some excellent fruit and veg from *Ted's Veg* with seasonal British produce and *Brockmans*

Farm for organic and biodynamic alternatives. The street might be relatively small, but you could do most of your week's shopping here with fresh organic meats, poultry and game, a selection of deli stalls with artisan food from across the UK and Europe including *Paté Moi* and their award winning mushroom paté, *Cannon & Cannon* with British cured salamis and chorizo, *Hook & Son* for raw organic dairy, French breads by *Olivier's Bakery* and, if you can fit it all in, pastries and cakes from specialist retailers such as the fabulous *Bad Brownie* and *Comptoir Gourmand*. The fresh fish and shellfish from Dorset's *Portland Scallop Co* are also well worth adding to your shopping basket. Amongst all the food there are in addition a few handmade craft and plant stalls.

Venn Street is not only a good place to source your weekly groceries, but also somewhere to relax and enjoy some top quality street food including delicious hog roast sandwiches courtesy of the local *Moen & Sons* butchers and freshly made Japanese dumplings from *The Gyoza Guys*. No account of Venn Street would be complete without mention of the long established flower stall at the top of the street, that offers great quality cut flowers, potted plants and succulents.

Southeast

Bermondsey Antiques Market

Bermondsey Square, between Abbey Street, Bermondsey Street and Tower Bridge Street, SE1 3UN
Tube: Borough, London Bridge (Northern)
Rail: London Bridge
Open: Fridays 6am-2pm

Bermondsey is London's oldest antiques market with origins dating back to before the war, when it traded in a square off Caledonian Road in Islington, which is why some still call it 'New Caledonian Market'. Visiting the market today is still a fascinating experience and many of the traders are old timers that have been selling their antiques and collectables here for many years and can tell you about when the market traded from a rough piece of wasteland that once occupied this site. In recent years the area has been transformed into a smart pedestrian square surrounded by modern flats and offices. David has been trading at Bermondsey since 1983 and looks on the changes with some scepticism, 'Some people call it progress... I don't!' He tells me, while still keeping a smile on his face.

There is some dissonance between the traditional antiques market and its modern location, but the place still has charm and some vestige of its history that makes it unique and still brings tourists from around the world seeking rare antiquities and collectables. The tourists usually arrive at their own leisurely pace around mid-morning, unaware that most of the serious antique dealing has taken place at the crack of dawn – or even by torch light in the winter months. The early morning trade can involve serious money being exchanged for silverware, jewellery, clocks, glassware, prints, china and porcelain, with a good deal of scrutinising and haggling between traders long familiar with each other and not afraid to argue.

It's less tense and more friendly as the morning wears on and it's always fun to visit and observe people from around the world haggle over the value of an item without the aid of a common language. The traders vary from dedicated specialists who can talk at length about their stock and its value, to more general dealers in all kinds of things from Dinky toys to old dental equipment and jewellery. Some of the traders are professionals who also trade at other antique markets in and around London, while a few of the characters here are semi-retired and trade as much for the fun as to make a living.

The downturn in the antiques trade generally and the upheavals the market has faced in past years have taken a toll, but Bermondsey Market is still a unique and special place and one well worth visiting, if only to get a glimpse into another and very different world.

Eat & Drink

There is a catering van on site which serves coffee and snacks and further afield is the famous *M.Manze* pie and mash shop at 87 Tower Bridge Road and next to them is the very good *Sobo* café. In the other direction there are several fashionable eateries and cafés on Bermondsey Street.

Southeast

Borough Market

Southwark Street, SE1 1TL

www.boroughmarket.org.uk

Twitter/Instagaram: @boroughmarket

Tube/Rail: London Bridge (Northern, Jubilee)

Open: Monday-Tuesday 10am-5pm (partially open), Wednesday-Thursday 10am-5pm, Friday till 6pm and Saturday 8am-5pm (full market)

It is hard to believe that back in 1994, Borough was a wholesale fruit and vegetable market where members of the public seldom set foot as the restaurateurs and caterers went about their business. Since then the market has undergone an incredible transformation, becoming one of Europe's leading food markets with thousands of visitors each day and many fashionable restaurants, cafés and specialist food outlets such as *Monmouth Coffee Company* and the *Neal's Yard Dairy* establishing themselves in the narrow roads around the old market. The transformation began with just a few stalls offering quality food at the weekend. Pioneers such as the wild boar farmer Peter Gott struggled as the market found its feet but soon persuaded others to join them as the venture acquired momentum. In the years that followed, the trustees of the market developed and improved the site with the help of architects *Greig + Stephenson* while still preserving the Art Deco exterior on Borough High Street and the 19th century wrought iron structure of the wholesale market. The changes included the expansion of the market into a canopied area between Bedale Street and Southward Cathedral – enabling over 100 additional food stalls to do business here.

Borough has flourished, becoming a remarkably vibrant food market with all kinds of retailers selling fresh food from around the globe. Here you can find meat sold direct from a single producer such as *Rhug Estate Farm*, as well as butchers like *Ginger Pig* selling high quality meat sourced from a number of farms. The cheese stalls are equally varied with *Kappacasein Dairy* offering their own London produced cheeses and yoghurt while the established *Une Normande à Londres* French delicatessen sell all kinds of cheeses, sausages and other produce. The fruit and vegetables are also exceptional with commercial greengrocers selling produce from around the world alongside specialist stalls. At a supermarket you might be lucky to find two or three kinds of mushroom, but at Borough there are over 20 types of fungi available from dried ceps to the gigantic puffball. Fishmongers are rarely found at most markets these days, but here there are several elaborate stalls selling anything from sea urchins and eel to more familiar staples like cod and salmon. Breads and patisserie are another of Borough's strengths with big names such as *Bread Ahead*, *Karaway Bakery* and *Olivier's Bakery* all regulars at the market.

The wine and beer traders include the renowned *Borough Wines* and *Utobeer* which offers over 600 different beers from around the world. Other traders, such as *New Forest Cider*, chose to simply sell their own product. The one thing all these dealers have in common is the use of small tasters, which is the ideal opportunity to try before you buy.

The atmosphere at Borough Market is infectious with crowds milling from stall to stall, sampling the food and chatting with the stall holders. It's now the unrivalled food market of the capital and one that appears to be going from strength to strength. It produces its own magazine – *Market Life* – with features and recipes inspired by the market and its traders. Visitors should also look out for the Market Hall where there is seating to enjoy your food and regular cookery demonstrations by well-known chefs. It's a great way to round off a visit to this incredible Mecca to food.

Eat & Drink

In a market dedicated to food there are countless opportunities to indulge your tastebuds with the canopied market, adjacent to Southwark Cathedral, the best place for street food with anything from delicious Egyptian vegan dishes at *Koshari St* to substantial meaty sandwiches from long established Borough Market favourites, *Roast Hog*. If you want to sit down and eat, there are plenty of great restaurants and cafés in and around the market with *Monmouth Coffee Company* on Stoney Street one of the best for coffee. *Maria's Café* in the heart of the market is great for traditional British grub.

Visit

There are all kinds of things to enjoy in the area with Tate Modern just a 10 minutes walk from here. On Saturdays you should make an effort to visit the fabulous Flea @ Flat Iron Sq (see page 215).

LEWISHAM COLLEGE CAR PARK
LEWISHAM WAY
LONDON
SE4 1UT

WWW.BROCKLEYMARKET.COM

BROCKLEY MARKET

SATURDAYS   10AM-2PM

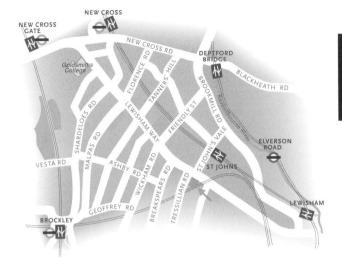

Brockley

Lewisham College Car Park, Lewisham Way, SE4 1UT
www.brockleymarket.com
Twitter: @BrockleyMarket
Instagram: @brockleymarket
Rail/Overground St Johns or Brockley
Open: Saturday 10am-2pm

This award-winning food market has a loyal following among the Brockley locals who manage to fill the car park of Lewisham College every Saturday come rain or shine, turning this little venture into a major feature of London's food landscape.

The customers are drawn by a great mix of food producers and street food stalls that make this a market to do both your weekly shop as well as relax and enjoy some great al fresco dining. For those after ingredients for the kitchen there are a number of organic fruit and veg stalls offering seasonal produce direct from

the farm. Brockley also boasts a quality fishmonger in *Veasey &
Sons*, who always have a great display of freshly-caught produce
and will gut and fillet to order as well as offering the odd cooking
tip. Carnivores will not be disappointed with several meat and
poultry stalls offering a limited but top quality selection, including
great bacon from Bermondsey based *The Butchery* and *Moons
Green Charcuterie* offering hand-carved ham to order. Cheese is
also an important part of the market with expert cheesemongers
Mons selling all kinds of artisan products with lots of tasters for
the curious. *Blackwoods Cheese Company* actually make a range of
their own unpasteurised cheeses and the deli stall *Flavours of Spain*
offers among its carefully-chosen selection of Spanish foods several
great cheeses including an award-winning manchego. Delicious
pickles, olives, breads, cakes and pastries as well as a selection of
locally brewed beers complete the picture and enable visitors to do a
complete shop here if needed.

Lovers of street food have plenty to choose from including great
sandwiches from *Sub Cult*, a bewildering selection of burgers from
Mother Flipper and a Vietnamese take on the same from *Bill or Beak*.
Dough Van have ingeniously managed to cram a wood burning stove
into a medium-sized van which sounds mad, but produces great
pizza. There's a seating area to enjoy the food and a great coffee
van from local café *Browns of Brockley* and *Good and Proper Tea*, if
you fancy something to drink. It's great to see this little foodie oasis
blossom in south east London – long may it continue.

Visit

If you fancy a bit of a market trawl, Lewisham Market (see page
229) is about 15 minutes to the east and is cheap and cheerful
and Deptford Market lies about 15 minutes to the south and
has a great second-hand and junk market on Douglas Way with
plenty of bargain vintage clothing (see page 205).

Southeast

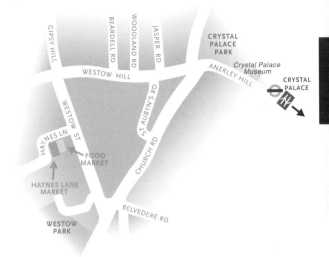

Crystal Palace Food Market

Haynes Lane, SE19 3AP
www.crystalpalacefoodmarket.co.uk
Twitter: @CPFoodMarket
Overground: Gypsy Hill or Crystal Palace
Open: Saturday 10am-3pm

Tucked away in a dilapidated group of courtyards off Westow Street and behind the large Sainsbury's, this food market is well worth seeking out. The Saturday market is part of the Transition Town movement and shares its ethos of supplying locally sourced and ethically produced food. Most produce comes from Sussex and Kent and some is even grown or produced in Crystal Palace through its patchwork of community growing spaces.

    The market might not be huge, but among the around 30 stalls you can find top quality meat from *Gill Wing Farm*, artisan cheeses, delicious cakes and pastries, an incredible range of fish from Sussex fishermen *Veasey & Sons* and fresh organic seasonal produce from *Wild Country Organics*, *Brambletye Fruit Farms* and *Brockmans Farm Produce*. In addition there are rotating olive and preserve stalls including flavourful and spicy sauces from London based *Chilli Bros* and homemade chutneys from *Creative Allsorts*. You can also taste and buy naturally produced wines, coffee roasted in London, gluten free treats, raw organic dairy, locally smoked meats and fish, as well as lunches from a host of street food stalls.

As if this wasn't enough, the market has its own little shop, *The Store Cupboard*, a no-waste refill shop offering a wide range of food staples, alongside another little shop, *Roots and Cycles*, who offer eco cleaning refills and organic beauty products as well as upcycled items. There are also a few arts and crafts traders setting up here offering an interesting choice of locally made original textiles and things for the home. The picture framer and art seller is also a permanent feature of the market and well worth checking out.

A great food market with a real community spirit, Crystal Palace Food Market shares the site with the equally interesting second-hand and vintage Haynes Lane Market (see page 223), which only adds to the appeal of the place.

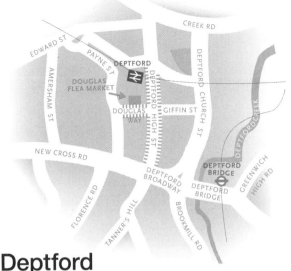

Deptford

Deptford High Street and Douglas Way SE8 4RT
Rail: Deptford, Deptford Bridge
Open: Wednesday, Friday and Saturday 8.30am-5pm

Deptford is just a fifteen minute bus ride from Greenwich, but it
has none of its famous neighbour's tourist attractions. Deptford's
market is huge, extending over half the length of Deptford High
Street and including a large flea market along Douglas Way and
Douglas Square. A visitor to Deptford can do all the weekly
essential shopping, but also indulge in the hunt for inexpensive
bric-à-brac. Markets that offer this kind of interesting shopping
are rare and Deptford is one of the best in the capital. In contrast
to the relatively ramshackle flea market, through the archway at
the far end of Douglas Square is *Deptford Market Yard* (www.
deptfordmarketyard.com) – a great space with smart independent
boutiques and cafés with outdoor seating on fine days.

Deptford High Street

The main thoroughfare of the market has over 100 stalls offering a great selection of basics like fresh fruit and veg, fresh fish, street fashion, bags and shoes, toiletries and household goods, perfume, watches, pet food and accessories. The market also has some outstanding specialist stalls dealing in car accessories and household blinds. The top end of the market even has a trader selling beds, with a choice of eight styles standing on the pavement. As well as beds you can also find other unusual things here like giant cooking pans that could feed a small village and one of London's last stalls specialising in net curtains. Food is not one of the market's strong points, but there are enough good fruit and veg stalls to allow visitors to stock up on good value produce, although the range is limited. The fresh fish stall is the most interesting food trader on the market with plenty of choice and the novelty of large cat fish swimming around in a shallow tank awaiting their fate. The main market has declined a little in the last ten years, but this period has seen an expansion of the flea market to become one of the best in London.

Douglas Flea Market

Deptford Square and Douglas Way

Flea markets have been under threat as their sites have given way to luxury flats and shops in places like Greenwich and Brick Lane. The decline has given a boost to those that are still going strong and Deptford Flea has definitely flourished in recent years and now trades on all market days and has expanded from its original site on Douglas Square and now extends all along Douglas Way on Saturdays. Here you can find about 60 stalls offering a sprawling assortment of bric-à-brac, bikes, used clothing, electrical goods, DVDs, jewellery and furniture. Most of the stalls on Douglas Square make no attempt at display with boxes of assorted items just put on the floor. Piles of books are stacked on stalls and pavement and sold for just a few pennies and there are many larger items like lawn mowers and hi-fi systems sold for just a fiver – but without any guarantee except the word of the trader. The clothing here is sold in a similarly chaotic manner with mountains of garments to sift through and most sold for just £1. The traders that now ply their wares on Douglas Way are more of a mix, with some ordered and tidy vintage clothing stalls among the chaos of second-hand bikes and hi-fi equipment. Christie is one of the regulars here and has several stalls which are a lot more organised, but also great value, with quality shirts for just a fiver and a great selection of washed and folded jeans for just a tenner.

Eat & Drink

Hullabaloo, on Douglas Way, is worth exploring for Indian vegan and vegetarian food. There are also lots of great eateries in Deptford Market Yard with our favourite being *Dirty Apron* in Arch 9 which does great food and has outdoor seating on fine days.

Visit

If the flea market hasn't exhausted your appetite for second-hand goods there are several excellent charity shops along the High Street and a very good vintage shop *Rag 'n' Bones* (140 Deptford High Street). If you like church architecture, St Paul's is a wonderful example of a baroque church at the north end of the market. Brockley Market is a great independent food market that trades on Saturdays and is just 15 minutes walk from here (see page 197).

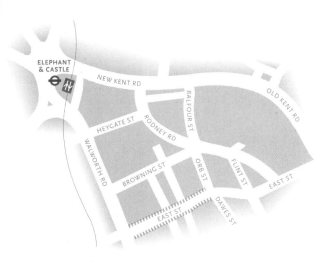

East Street

East Street between Walworth Road and Dawes Street, SE17 1EL
Tube: Elephant & Castle (Northern, Bakerloo)
Open: Tuesday-Sunday 8.30am-4pm (busiest at weekends, when
the street's shops are open both days)

The birthplace of Charlie Chaplin, East Street is also home to
one of South London's biggest, busiest and loudest markets. At
weekends, with stalls along the length of this long street, tides
of determined shoppers weave around clumps of slow-moving
bargain hunters as the queues build for cut-price essentials. The
market still has a bustling atmosphere, but the winds of change
are sweeping through the area as local estates such as the
Heygate are sold to developers and families are forced to leave
the area. The new arrivals are urban professionals who appear
to be far more likely to shop at supermarkets or online than to
negotiate the bustling East Street on a Saturday afternoon.

Despite these changes, there are still enough local people whose needs for the practical, wearable and edible give East Street a genuine sense of community, with lots of classic South London humour, a real mix of shoppers, plenty of banter and noisily competitive traders stoking the lively atmosphere. The traders are an important part of the community with many old characters having worked here since they were spring chickens. The market isn't a wise choice for the delicate or the hung-over, with lots of noise and bustle as thousands of people make their way between the stalls. On busy days you will need to watch out for serious jostlers, and East Street can also bring new meaning to the phrase 'price wars' as you get caught in the crossfire between sellers as phrases like 'Oi! Come on, who wants a bargain?', 'Two pounds of mush' a nicker' are bellowed for all to hear. But the demonstrations of iron-larynxed stamina and word-mangling delivery make brilliant free entertainment.

The size of the market means that rival traders have to compete on price, so make sure you don't part with your cash without first checking out the competition. East Street is surprisingly long and from its start on Walworth Road it's quite a trek to the far end, at the junction with Dawes Street. The market offers all the staples, with lots of great bargains for the discerning shopper amongst piles of household and electrical goods, bedding, sweets, luggage, perfume, toiletries, jewellery, toys, fruit and veg (from the Caribbean as well as the UK), plants and flowers. The local Chinese community are also beginning to make their presence felt on the market with some very fine Oriental handbags for only £7 and another stall offering Chinese medicine including tea that claims to help discourage smoking.

Certain things do stand out. East Street is full of clothes, and many of the shops and stalls offer impressive reductions on chain store prices – underwear, dresses, and shirts are often good value – although sifting is essential as much of the stock is definitely more cheap and cheerful than chic. At the far end of the market are several stalls offering piles of High Street seconds for just £1 a garment and these are always busy with local bargain hunters. A number of haberdashery and material stalls also offer D.I.Y. fashion bunnies the chance to create some pretty snazzy outfits. The shoe stalls also carry a wide range with some persuasive prices, like the one selling piles of women's leather sandals for just £4 a pair.

Just ten years ago there used to be six large stalls offering cut flowers and bedding plants, but now the Edge family are the last of the plant sellers on the street. Despite the downturn in trade they still keep smiling as one of them told me 'We've cornered the market in flowers round 'ere; lot of good it's done us!'

East Street might be facing the problems of gentrification, but it's still a great place to visit and a throwback to a time when local street markets were at the heart of any London community.

Eat & Drink

There are several street food stalls along the market with the jerk chicken stall a firm favourite with the locals. Many of the greasy spoons along East Street have disappeared in recent years but *Jack's Café* (at 81a) is still gong strong and worth a visit. A new arrival is *55 East* which is run as a social enterprise and offers regular events and a community space, as well as hot food, snacks and great coffee.

Elephant & Castle

Outside Elephant & Castle shopping centre ,SE1
www.elephantmarket.com
Tube: Elephant & Castle (Northern and Bakerloo)
Rail: Elephant & Castle (Blackfriars)
Open: Monday-Saturday 9.30am-5pm

This market has been circling the famous Elephant and Castle
shopping centre at below ground level for over 20 years,
which is about the last time the centre received a lick of paint.
Unfortunately, its location – stuck under the centre's concrete
petticoats – hasn't helped to establish much of an atmosphere.
People surfacing from the labyrinthine tunnels under the
Elephant's twin roundabouts seem mainly concentrated on their
journey, and few stop to check out the 20 or so stalls that set
up here. The selection of goods on offer is pretty uninspiring,
focusing on new clothes, sportswear, accessories, jewellery,

watches, toys, household goods and toiletries, but there are a few genuine bargains such as quality cloth caps for just a fiver.

On the sartorial front, some stalls stock slightly more interesting and fashionable women's clothes, but the emphasis is on cheap, functional separates aimed generally at a more middle-aged customer. A few traders have £1 rails or jumble-style tables with mixes of second-hand clothes, but there are few choice items in amongst the nylon nasties of yesteryear. The large shoe stall has some reasonable deals, with brand name trainers for around £25. One of the characters of the market is Alan, otherwise known as the Vinyl Vagabond, who sells old records for anything from £1 to £500, as well as assorted second-hand gear.

Eat & Drink

There isn't much in the way of eateries on the market, but John offers good coffee and waffles at his *Black Cowboy* stall. Veggies and vegans might like to try *Cupcakes and Shhht* which is located in a complex of container units called *The Artworks* behind the shopping centre.

Vintage and Makers Market Every Saturday and Sunday

Flat Iron Square
London SE1 1RU

flatironsquare.co.uk
@flea_flatironsquare

Flea @ Flat Iron Square

53 Southwark Street, SE1 1RU
www.fleaflatironsquare.co.uk
Twitter: @fleaflatironsquare
Instagram: flea_flatironsquare
Tube: London Bridge (Northern & Jubilee)
Rail: London Bridge
Open: Saturday 11am-6pm, Sunday 10am-5pm

Flat Iron Square Flea Market is a new addition to London's market
scene having opened its doors to the public for the first time in
the autumn of 2016. It may be a fresh-faced arrival, but it has the
feel of a market that has been here for years and is a real throw
back to the kind of friendly, great value second-hand market that
looked threatened by London's property boom.

Flea markets have always thrived on undeveloped land
and Flat Iron is no exception, taking place on what was once a

rough square of land that was used as a car park and has now been transformed into a lush garden with a bar and outdoor garden stage. It is here that about thirty traders set up, offering a mixed bag of vintage clothing, bric-à-brac, furniture and even a few designer-makers selling things like unique cotton socks and toiletries.

One of the regulars here is Dinos, who has one of the largest pitches selling an assortment of renovated metal cabinets, second-hand clothing and other assorted homewares. He loves the market and was one of the first to start trading here:

> *'I'm really just an enthusiastic amateur. I collect stuff and so have to sell stuff to make room. The people are really friendly and I've got a lot of friends among the other traders. Business is sometimes good, sometimes not so good, but I always enjoy myself and that's what keeps me coming back..'*

Relaxing in his hanging wicker chair and sipping from a small glass of whisky, it's obvious that Dinos is enjoying the experience.
Just a few pitches away from Dinos is Paul, who is a natty model for his collection of retro men's clothing including some very fine tweed jackets for as little as £20, some great vintage cufflinks and even a number of old radios and record players.

Once you've had enough shopping, walk through to the railway arches where there are a number of permanent restaurants with outdoor seating as well as a few street food traders offering all kinds of delicious grub.

Visit
There are all kinds of things to enjoy in the area with Tate Modern not far from here. For market junkies, just a few minutes walk from Flat Iron is the fabulous Borough Market (see page 191).

'I'm really just an enthusiastic amateur. I collect stuff and so have to sell stuff to make room. The people are really friendly and I've got a lot of friends among the other traders. Business is sometimes good, sometimes not so good, but I always enjoy myself and that's what keeps me coming back..'

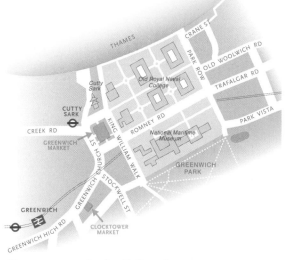

Greenwich Market

Entrances on Greenwich Church Street, College Approach,
King William Walk and Nelson Road, SE10 9HZ
Food court on Durnford Street
www.greenwichmarketlondon.com
Twitter: @greenwichmkt
Rail/ Overground: Greenwich
Open: Daily 10am-5pm
Monday-Tuesday, Friday (vintage, art and crafts, street food),
Wednesday (crafts and food), Thursday (vintage and food),
Saturday-Sunday (arts and crafts & food)

This covered market in the heart of Greenwich is one of London's
oldest, having acquired a royal charter in 1700 – although in those
days it traded in wholesale fruit and veg rather than the arts, crafts,
collectables and fine food that are sold here today. The buildings
around the central courtyard complement the market and the cobbled

stones and original paving give this place a real old world charm. Some things have changed over the years with the addition of a glass roof that has been keeping out the elements since the 1980s and the recently built modern food court just off Durnford Street.

In recent years the street food part of the market has really taken off with about a quarter of the market now dedicated to foodie delights, with lots of street food traders at the College Approach entrance to the market and the new food court offering anything from hefty beef sandwiches to freshly prepared vegan food.

At the weekend the market is a really good mix of genuine craft goods with unique bags, plant pots, clothing, soft toys and art work. Some of the larger markets in London can be a bit generic, but at Greenwich there are many original products – most of them sold by the designer-makers. A recent visit found a seller of succulents who actually grew her own plants and made the pots they were sold in, a young trader selling bags made from recycled material that she had expertly sewn and a clothing designer offering a great selection of original skirts and tops. Amidst all this youthful enthusiasm there is an elderly gent called Kurt, who has been selling leather goods here for donkey's years, but recently added a great choice of second-hand books to his stall which attracts attention from passing bookworms.

While this market is at its busiest and best at the weekend, it trades throughout the week – the Wednesday craft market and Thursday vintage market are particularly good and well worth a visit if you fancy a slightly less hectic shopping experience.

Eat & Drink

One of the best things about this market is its relaxed atmosphere and loads of places to eat and drink. Among the place to sit and relax with a pint are *The Coach and Horses* and *Admiral Hardy* pubs. The food courts offer food from around the world and there are benches to sit and enjoy your food on Durnford Street.

Clock Tower Market
Greenwich High Road (next to the Greenwich Cinema)
www.clocktowermarket.co.uk
Twitter: @clocktower_mkt
Open: Saturday-Sunday 10am-5pm

Greenwich has changed a good deal over the last 20 years, but the Clock Tower Market remains very much as it was back in the day. The courtyard is open to the elements, but there's always a reasonable selection of collectables, antiques, vinyl, jewellery, books and vintage fashion to sift through at the weekend.

The customers are quite a mix with young students from the University looking for cheap vintage fashion, rubbing shoulders with elderly couples on the hunt for antiques. The market is a great place to look for interesting jewellery and there is always a good choice of books, vinyl, CDs and DVDs for those that have steadfastly refused to go down the digital route for their entertainment. Just a few minutes from the main Greenwich shopping area, the Clock Tower Market is well worth a visit.

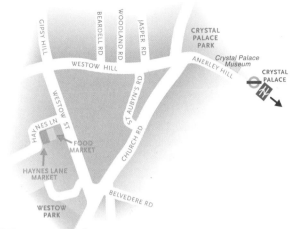

Haynes Lane

Haynes Lane, SE19 3AN
Twitter: @Hayneslanemkt
Rail/Overground: Gypsy Hill or Crystal Palace
Open: Friday & Sunday 11am-5pm, Saturday 10.30-5pm
Located in old workshops behind Sainsbury's, this little market is
a great place to rummage for antiques, collectables and good old
fashioned junk. The old workshops that have become home to
the market are a little chaotic, but that's part of its charm. Among
the interesting things to be found here are all kinds of discarded
toys and figurines, one trader dealing in books and DVDs and on
the first floor there is a unit dedicated to vintage clothing. There
are also a few more selective 20th-century vintage specialists with
some genuinely collectable furniture at reasonable prices. This
little market is a good place to while away an hour and you're sure
to emerge with something interesting to treasure from a Penguin
paperback to a genuine 1960s coffee table. The market is best
visited on a Saturday when the outside courtyards are the site for the
wonderful Crystal Palace Food Market (see page 201).

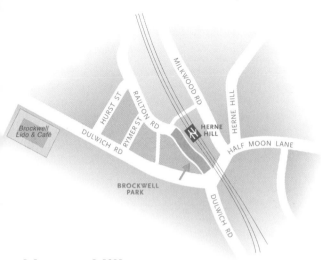

Herne Hill
Farmers' Market

Railton Road, Herne Hill, SE24 0JN

www.weareccfm.com

Twitter: @hernehillmarket

Rail: Herne Hill

Open: Sunday 10am-4pm

Herne Hill Market has emerged from nowhere in the last five years and is now one of the best in London. It takes place every Sunday on a small stretch of Railton Road just outside Herne Hill station. The market is a fraction of the size of giants like Brick Lane or Portobello Road, but the fifty or so stalls that set up here manage to provide everything visitors need for a weekly shop as well as several unexpected surprises. One of the surprises is the bike repair stall (*Like Your Bike*) that offers services, repairs and parts and is always busy. The Dulwich Road end of the market has quite a few local designers selling their wares including *Wolle & Hide* who specialise in handmade wool clothing and leather accessories and *Stripey Squirrel* with their colourful range of kids' clothing. The cacti and indoor plant stall is also an unusual feature of the market with lots of healthy plants and pots and free advice for anyone needing it. There are also a few original jewellery stalls on the market with plenty of great value trinkets to sort through. Those looking for more practical work wear will not be disappointed with a regular trader offering smocks and clogs and several good stalls selling original street fashion. There are also a few bric-à-brac and collectable traders, a dealer in oriental rugs and throws and several art stalls including a selection from *Planet Patrol Pop Up Gallery*, and local artist Luke Adam Hawker who sells his fine drawings here and online.

Like east London's Broadway Market, Herne Hill is a good balance of gifts and food and it's possible to do a weekly shop here and get most of what you need, which is sure sign of a good market. Among the delicacies are delicious scotch eggs in all manner of flavours, fine Sicilian pastries, several stalls selling cured meats with lots of samples to try and a number of cheese sellers including the excellent *London Cheesemongers*. The stall offering fine jams was also worth a gander with plenty of tasters so you can try before you buy. Accompanying these fine foods are grocery essentials such as *Brockmans Organic Fruit and Veg*, several artisan bread and cake sellers and a choice of good butchers, plus fresh fish from the *Portland Scallops Co.*

Street food is an important part of most markets these days and Herne Hill has a great range of food to eat on the go including a great Moroccan food stall, one offering vast pans of hot and delicious French stews and another catering for vegans with tasty salad boxes.

It seems remarkable that such a vibrant and interesting market has blossomed in just a few years. With Herne Hill Station in the middle of the market it's easy to get to and one well worth making an effort to visit.

Visit

For literary types *Herne Hill Books* is at 289 Railton Road and
is open on Sundays. Just around the corner from the market
is a fabulous 20th Century furniture store called *Morbleu* and
for more junk and collectables there's the fabulously named
Society for the Protection of Unwanted Objects. Those who enjoy
outdoor swimming should pack their cossie because *Brockwell
Lido* is just around the corner in the grounds of the wonderful
Brockwell Park.

Eat & Drink

If you fancy a drink there are two good pubs in the area, *The
Commercial* (on the market) and *The Florence* (just around
the corner). For coffee and snacks there's *Milkwood Café* and
Blackbird Bakery.

Southeast

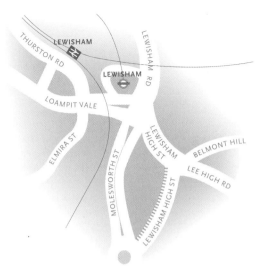

Lewisham High Street

North End of Lewisham High Street, SE13 6JG
Rail: Lewisham, Lewisham DLR or Ladywell
Open: Monday-Saturday 9am-5pm (food, household goods and
clothing), Sunday 9am-5pm (household goods,
fashion and street food)

Lewisham market is as much a part of the landscape as the town
clock which marks its beginning and the tower of St Saviour's
Church which can be seen in the distance. In truth the most
prominent feature of the area is the Lewisham Centre which
provides a backdrop to a friendly street market that offers a
good selection of street clothing, fruit and veg, cut flowers and
household goods to the locals that have the good sense to avoid
the local supermarkets. The fish stall has a limited range of
fishy delights, but with bargains like five sea bream for a tenner
it's hard to complain. During the week the majority of stalls are

dedicated to fruit and veg with all kinds of produce to choose from and some of the lowest prices to be found in the capital. Tom's family has been selling fruit and veg here for over 100 years and he has seen a few changes:

> 'People now want everything in a bowl for a pound. It didn't used to be that way, but now if I put two aubergine out and no one wants 'em, stick 'em in a bowl for a quid and it sells.. I don't get people sometimes.'

Lewisham Market is probably not worth going out of your way to visit, but it is great value and still has an atmosphere and friendliness that few other London markets can match. On Sundays the market is slightly different and sells only household goods, clothing and street food.

Eat & Drink
On Lewis Grove (just behind the market) there are a few good places to get a bite to eat including *Antonio Delicatessen*, *Bella Roma* Italian restaurant and the *Market Café* for hearty British grub. Just around the corner at 2 Rennell Street is the wonderful *Sparrow* restaurant which is always busy.

Visit
On Saturdays you can combine a visit to Lewisham with a very different market experience at Brockley Market which is about 15 minutes walk from here (see page 197)

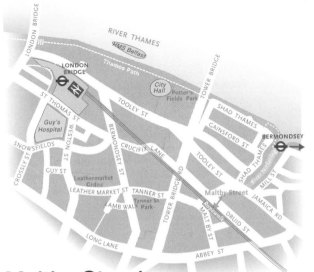

Maltby Street

37 Maltby Street, Rope Walk, SE1 3PA
www.maltbystmarket.co.uk
Twitter: @MaltbyStMkt
Tube/Rail: London Bridge (Northern, Jubilee),
Bermondsey (Jubilee)
Open: Saturday 9am-4pm, Sunday 11am-4pm

Rope Walk might only be a hundred metres long but every weekend within the narrow confines of this pedestrian walkway you can find mouth-watering food from around the world. Although the path is fairly tucked away, it's easy to find as the surrounding streets are always crowded with visitors enjoying all kinds of delicacies from spicy burgers to steaming portions of veggie Indo-Persian curry.

Having found your way to the market it's a good idea to stroll through and see everything before getting stuck in. Every taste and dietary requirement is catered for; from the strict vegan to the dyed-in-the-wool carnivore. Likewise, the food is international with French patisserie, Asian wraps, Japanese gyoza and Mexican burritos all competing for your culinary attention; not to mention good British fare like Scotch eggs and the popular Beef Steaks stall.

The sweet-toothed will also not be disappointed with lots of delicious treats such as freshly made waffles alongside the long established and very delicious *Bad Brownie* stall with fine patisserie provided by *Comptoir Gourmand*.

Visitors looking for something liquid to accompany their food are spoilt for choice with the *Modern Beer Bar* and *Old Bermondsey Brewery* all represented as well as *Craft Coffee* and *Bumpin' Rinds* juice bar offering non-alcoholic options.

The fact that Malby Street is teeming with hungry foodies even on the wettest of weekends is testament to the incredible interest in great street food in the capital – long may it continue!

North Cross Road

North Cross Rd (from Lordship Lane to Fellbrigg Rd), SE22 9ET
Rail: East Dulwich
Open: Saturdays 10am-5pm

There's been a market on North Cross Road for years, but it has experienced its ups and downs over that time and has survived by adapting to the now prosperous neighbourhood – good-bye cheap fruit and veg, hello hand-made pouffes. The longest-serving stall on the market belongs to fishmonger, Jeff Bowman, who has been selling top quality fresh fish here for over 35 years and has witnessed the transformation. Jeff trades on the corner of Lordship Lane from Thursday, but he only has company on Saturdays, when another 20 stalls line the street offering anything from reconditioned furniture to farm fresh eggs.

The market now has a regular following, drawn here by the appealing mix of the practical, the unusual and the beautiful. The egg stall is always here offering a selection of free range eggs from all manner of fowl. It's not unusual to have a plant stall at a market, but the regular one here is run by *Cade Street Nursery* and sells plants that are incredibly lush and healthy. If you're looking for a gift or just to treat yourself there are plenty of options, from scented candles by *Aequill* to jewellery from long established trader *Lisa E Moss*. Further along the market there's a mix of vintage and second-hand stalls and three wonderful crafts people – Alice King and her hand-made ceramics, Kate Diamond and her own range of T-shirts and *Tuffet.co*, the aforementioned pouffes, which are expensive, but truly things of beauty. If you've come on your bike, don't forget the bike repair stall at the Lordship Lane end of the market. There are quite a few food stalls here offering things like hand-made chocolates and artisan breads, but the majority of food is to eat on the go, including burritos and hog roast sandwiches.

North Cross Road has a great atmosphere and it's clear that the traders and customers really value the place. There are plans to extend the number of stalls and pedestrianise more of the street on Saturdays – a sign that this market is still looking to the future.

Eat & Drink

Good cafés along the North Cross Road include *Bonne Bouffe* at number 49 and further up at number 18 the *Blue Mountain Café*. *The Palmerston* (on Lordship Lane) has a great menu.

Visit

The fabulous independent bookshop, *Rye Books*, has relocated to 47 North Cross Road and not only offers a great selection of books but also has a lovely little coffee shop. Further afield, The Horniman Museum and Dulwich Picture Gallery are both just a bus ride away and are well worth exploring.

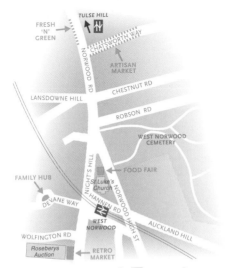

West Norwood Feast

Norwood Road and Knight's Hill, SE27 0HS

Rail: West Norwood or Tulse Hill

www.westnorwoodfeast.com

Twitter: @WN_FEAST

Instagram: WN_FEAST

Open: First Sunday of month April to December 10am-4pm

What makes this market special is the involvement of the West Norwood community with lots of talented local designer-makers, caterers, charities and vintage traders taking a stall. The event is managed by an enthusiastic team and on market days an army of blue high-vis jacketed volunteers are on-hand to offer help and direct visitors to the market's four locations.

Most people visiting the market from outside the area will arrive at West Norwood overground station and will immediately encounter the 'Family hub', by the leisure centre, where there are free children's activities, an open mic performance space for young people and stalls offering a mix of kids' T-shirts, handmade soaps and make-up and a local artists selling their own work. If you get peckish there are a handful of street food stalls.

Further up Knights Hill, in the car park of an auction house, there is the 'Retro Village' were all kinds of vintage clothing, household goods, second-hand books and accessories can be found among the 15 or so stalls.

After visiting the Retro Market head down the hill to the courtyard of the St Luke's church, where most of the street food is concentrated with delicious treats from around the world from Greek wraps and Indian curry to traditional fare, such as burgers and freshly baked sausage rolls. This part of the market is also where a lot of the entertainment takes place with local bands playing at the entrance to the church.

Further down, Chatsworth Way hosts the small but charming Artisan Market where about 20 designer-makers offer original art work, cushions and throws, stylish crockery and kitchenware, kids' clothes, T-shirts for grown-ups, all kinds of jewellery and lots of great cards. The traders are nearly all selling their own products or designs and are always keen to chat about their work, with some undertaking commissions and bespoke services if needed.

The last part of the market is just opposite, on Norwood Road, where a handful of quality food producers set out their wares including locally produced honey, a great fish stall, handmade chocolates and a stall offering beers from London's burgeoning micro-brewery scene. There's even a few deli stalls selling anything from fine cured meats, delicious olives and a good choice of artisan cheeses.

West Norwood is not a place that attracts many visitors from outside the area, but this market is a real gem and well worth taking the trouble to visit, if only to see how a market can thrive when supported by the local community.

EAST

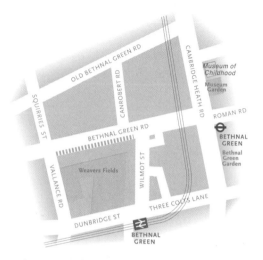

Bethnal Green Road

Bethnal Green Road (Vallance Road to Wilmot Street), E2
Tube: Bethnal Green (Central Line)
Open: Monday-Saturday 8.30am-5pm,
Thursday 8.30am-12.30pm

There has been a market on Bethnal Green Road since the 19th century, and despite the arrival of a Tescos and the neglect of the local council, it's still going strong. The market is an expression of the East End's continued vitality and on any weekday you will see East Enders rubbing shoulders with Asian and African locals, as well as more recent arrivals from Eastern Europe. The atmosphere is friendly with plenty of banter as traders chat with their regulars.

Bethnal Green Road provides everything you might need, from bedding to plugs and generally of reliable quality. There is nothing out of the ordinary here, but if you're after a relaxed, no frills, market then this one should fit the bill.

Norman, the last of the old East End fruit and veg men, sold his last apple back in 2016, but there are still a good few grocery stalls on the market, now offering a more mixed assortment of the everyday and the exotic to cater for the local Asian community with mooli, tinda and Okra all piled high and sold cheap.

Bethnal Green has a few clothes stalls, with a spectrum of new men's and women's clothing ranging from middle-aged and functional to casual jeans and jackets. Prices are often, to quote one trader's sign, 'Bloody Cheap!', and there are indeed plenty of solid bargains. One of the longest established traders is Pam's pet food stall. Pam has been selling all kinds of things for your furry friend since 1971. After over 40 years of trading she's seen a lot of change, but still enjoys the market and its people.

Bethnal Green is one of the last fully functioning weekday markets that has not succumbed to the tidal wave of street food. There are signs that things are changing and one or two of the old faces have left the market, but this part of town still seems to have a local community that value and use their local market – let's hope it continues that way.

Eat & Drink

G.Kelly (414 Bethnal Green Road) serves pie and mash in a textbook marble and benches interior, while E.Pellici is a classic Italian caff which has been on the site since 1900. At the heart of the market is Café 338 which is very popular and has outside seating. At the Cambridge Heath end of the market is a nice little café called Munch Munch.

Visit

The main attraction in this part of town is The Museum of Childhood which is on Cambridge Heath Road and is a great place to take children of all ages.

East

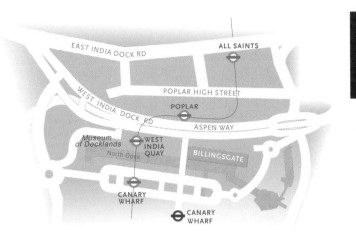

Billingsgate

North quay of West India Dock, Isle of Dogs, E14 5ST
Tube: Canary Wharf (Jubilee)
DLR: West India Quay
Open: Tuesday-Saturday 4am-8.30am

Billingsgate fish market moved to this modern warehouse
in January 1982 from its City location in Lower Thames
Street, where it had been trading for nearly a thousand years.
Billingsgate's new premises lack the grandeur of the old building
(which was designed by Sir Horace Jones) but, given the
commercial nature of the market and the volume of traffic in the
City, such a pragmatic move was inevitable. The new market,
although ugly from the outside, still has a great atmosphere and
continues the great tradition of London's fish trade.

A stone's throw away from Canary Wharf, the market is easy
to find – one dead giveaway are the seagulls which constantly

circle above, some of whom have grown huge on the fishy titbits so readily in supply. Billingsgate also has its own seal, called *Sammy*, who resides in the dock at the back of the market and is fed by the porters on salmon heads.

The market is busiest between 4am and 6am, when most of the commercial buyers are doing business – haggling over prices and checking the quality of the stock. Some of the traders are wholesale only, but it's worth asking, as many will sell to individual customers and newcomers are always given a friendly welcome. It's a great place to come with a recipe in mind and hunt down the freshest ingredients possible – just watch out for the forklift trucks operating at the entrance to the market.

Among the fifty or so traders you can find every kind of fish imaginable, such as white sturgeon, spotted dogfish and large catfish. There's also a comprehensive selection of crustaceans and molluscs with anything from deep-water shrimps to live lobsters with their pincers bound to prevent an unwelcome nip.

If you don't fancy getting up at some unspeakable hour to hunt down the best fish at Billingsgate, there is a man that will do all the graft for you. Markymarket (www.markymarket.com / Twitter @markymarket) visits both Smithfield and Billingsgate Markets several times a week and delivers straight to your door.

Eat & Drink
There are two caffs on the premises but they cater largely for the porters and although you will be made to feel welcome, you will need to tolerate the ever-present aroma of fish.

Brick Lane Bookshop

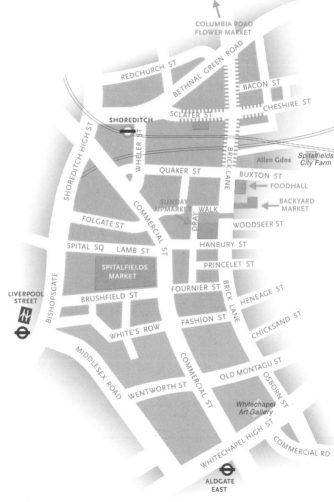

COLUMBIA ROAD
FLOWER MARKET

REDCHURCH ST

BETHNAL GREEN ROAD

BACON ST

CHESHIRE ST

SHOREDITCH

SCLATER ST

SHOREDITCH HIGH ST

WHELER ST

BRICK LANE

Allen Gdns

Spitalfields
City Farm

QUAKER ST

BUXTON ST

FOODHALL

COMMERCIAL ST

SUNDAY
UPMARKET

DRAY WALK

BACKYARD
MARKET

FOLGATE ST

WOODSEER ST

SPITAL SQ

LAMB ST

HANBURY ST

SPITALFIELDS
MARKET

PRINCELET ST

BISHOPSGATE

BRUSHFIELD ST

FOURNIER ST

BRICK LANE

HENEAGE ST

LIVERPOOL
STREET

WHITE'S ROW

FASHION ST

CHICKSAND ST

MIDDLESEX ROAD

COMMERCIAL ST

OLD MONTAGU ST

OSBORN ST

WENTWORTH ST

Whitechapel
Art Gallery

WHITECHAPEL HIGH ST

COMMERCIAL RD

ALDGATE
EAST

248   East

Brick Lane

Brick Lane (Bethnal Green Road to Hanbury Street), Bethnal
Green Road (from Brick Lane to Commercial Street) and Sclater
Street, E1-E2
Tube: Liverpool Street (Metro & Circle Lines), Aldgate East
(District), Old Street (Northern), Shoreditch High Street (East
London Line)
Open: Sunday 6am-1pm (Street Market),
Thursday-Friday 11am-5.30pm, Saturday 11am-6pm,
Sunday 10am-5pm (Vintage Market)
Sunday 10am-5pm (Sunday Upmarket)
Saturday 11am-6pm, Sunday 10am-5pm (The Backyard Market,
Boiler House Food Hall and The Tea Rooms)

With so many of London's markets being ordered to conform with
local government regulations, Brick Lane is a last bastion of disorder
and lawlessness and is all the better for it. In the last 20 years the
onward march of gentrification has seen several old courtyards that
were once key parts of the market give way to housing developments
and Cheshire Street, once one of the market's key thoroughfares, is
now very quiet on a Sunday with just a few stalls. These changes have
not diminished the market – where once Cheshire Street was busy,
now Brick Lane itself has become the centre of activity.

The area around Truman Brewery has in the last twenty years
become the heart of a more fashionable market with indoor spaces at
The Upmarket and Backyard Market. It's at these markets that East
London's small businesses and designers can sell direct to the public
and these have been joined in recent years by the busy Boiler House
Food Hall, Vintage Market and a smaller retail area called The Tea
Rooms. The different parts of the market are dealt with separately
below, but the market is always in a state of flux so always expect
some changes, particularly to the outdoor markets.

Brick Lane
(from Bethnal Green Road to Quaker St)

For a while back in the noughties, Brick Lane lost its vibe and had just a few stalls on a Sunday. It has now regained its mojo and is again the vibrant backbone of the market with a great range of stalls extending south from the junction with Bethnal Green Road. On the junction with Bethnal Green Road there are a few great value fruit and veg stalls and several bric-à-brac traders selling anything from old vinyl to vintage clocks, crockery and furniture. Describing this part of the market is always difficult as it changes from week to week, so be prepared for a few surprises.

As you walk further down Brick Lane, approaching the overhead railway bridge, the market changes from bric-à-brac to outdoor street food, with about 40 stalls setting up here on a Sunday offering anything from paella to pork sandwiches, fresh sushi to substantial bowls of pasta. As if this wasn't enough street food, just a bit further down is the Boiler House Food Hall (see below).

Boiler House Food Hall
152 Brick Lane next to Buxton Street
Twitter: @trumanbrewery
www.boilerhouse-foodhall.co.uk

This indoor food hall is easy to spot as it's just below the iconic Truman Brewery chimney which can be seen above the crowds all the way along Brick Lane. It's a great place to wander from stall to stall and sample food from around the world from halloumi and falafel wraps to Chinese bao buns served warm and fresh from their bamboo steamers. Among the 60 or so stalls you are bound to find something tempting and there is plenty here for vegans, vegetarians and those with a sweet tooth. The Boiler House also has a back garden which is a great place to relax with your food on fine days and there's a beer garden if you're thirsty.

East

Bethnal Green Road
(from Sclater Street to Commercial Street)
Bethnal Green Road is where many of the itinerant traders set out their wares. Here you can find an odd assortment of second-hand clothes, bric-à-brac, books, CDs and vinyl, cameras and bikes. Street hawkers and fly traders are part of the character and history of Brick Lane and although they move around, they are well worth seeking out.

Sclater Street
(from Bethnal Green to Brick Lane)
The junction with Bethnal Green Road is where a large fruit and veg stall sets out ten tables piled high with fresh produce. The prices are dirt cheap and there are enough eager customers to keep six people busy until the market closes in the afternoon. As you proceed down Sclater Street you can find a dealer selling bike parts and a large stall specialising in DIY bits and pieces. Bargain hunters should look out for the archway shop selling good quality sheets and towels for just a few pounds.

Further along, just opposite the junction with Bacon Street, is one of the last remaining squares in the area with traders selling bikes and bike parts, CDs, vinyl, old clothes, bric-à-brac and used power tools, amid a ramshackle selection of about 30 stalls. This might seem chaotic and messy to some, but it is where many of the best bargains and unusual things can be found and is a real throwback to the old days of the market when there were several similar courtyards in the area.

Back on Sclater Street you can find a selection of stalls selling cheap bags, street fashion and discounted tinned and packaged food, but most importantly the man specialising in coffee sacks. This might sound a strange thing to make a business from, but there are 101 uses for a coffee sack – he even has a website (bricklanecoffeesacks.co.uk). At the junction with Brick Lane can be found the incredible chess man, who plays up to four games of chess with passing challengers and does so for fun. Further proof, if it were needed, that Brick Lane is a special place.

Bacon Street

Bacon Street has lost its famous courtyard, but there are still the old industrial units selling cheap household goods and another specialising in used commercial kitchen equipment, both run by old characters that have seen the area change around them, but still manage to smile and share a joke or two. On the junction with Sclater Street is a large vintage clothing stall with rail upon rail to sift through and plenty of discount gear for just a fiver.

Cheshire Street

Cheshire Street still has its share of vintage stores and the incredible *Blackman's Shoes* which has been there for over forty years, but the market has for the moment largely left the street. Things change and the market might well return to the street, such is the Hydra-like nature of Brick Lane.

Backyard Market

146 Brick Lane, E1 6RU
www.backyardmarket.co.uk
Open: Saturday 11-6pm and Sunday 10-5pm
This place is not difficult to find with several food stalls extending onto Brick Lane and funky music that can be heard from the street – played by the market's vinyl dealer who usually accompanies the tracks with a tambourine. This unprepossessing concrete warehouse is transformed at the weekend with about 80 stalls setting up here. On offer is a mix of independent designer clothes and gifts as well as several good value retro stalls. There is a far more arty and fashionable atmosphere here than at the more traditional parts of Brick Lane with dealers often attempting to sell original work and taking some care about the display of their wares. Among the retro clothing dealers there are some good bargains with several discounted rails offering garments reduced to clear for just £5. Hillary has been selling retro garments at Portobello on a Saturday for over 30 years, but is now also a regular here on a

Sunday – offering bargains like jeans for £10. One of my favourite stalls belonged to the collective of Japanese artists that were selling their own range of funny and sinister cards, postcards and jewellery for just a couple of pounds. The cappuccino stall at the front of the market is a good place to go for a caffeine boost if you need it. After desperately searching for some originality in Camden in recent weeks it is great to find so many interesting things here.

The Sunday Upmarket
(The Old Truman Brewery, entrances on Brick Lane, Hanbury Street and Wilkes Street)
www.sundayupmarket.co.uk
This vast indoor market is at the heart of Brick Lane's transformation with the formerly empty surrounding streets becoming shopping avenues with boutiques and cafés. The Sunday market itself occupies the Old Truman Brewery and holds about 150 stalls offering all kinds of arts and crafts, hand-made toys, new and retro clothing, jewellery, accessories, shoes and homewares. The stalls here are often organised and run with enthusiasm by the designers themselves, who nearly always have business cards and websites to promote their wares. One such stall is *IOMA*, selling their original range of street ware from baseball caps to T-shirts and tops. The Upmarket is also a good place to find original jewellery with designer-makers like *Lizzy Chambers* (lizzychambers. com) regulars here at the weekend. If you haven't had your fill of street food there are also a host of food stalls around the market. With so many good stalls attracting large crowds every weekend, the Upmarket seems destined to go from strength to strength. There are several umbilical corridors that connect the Upmarket with the more recent Vintage Market...

The Vintage Market

(Block F, The Old Truman Brewery, 85 Brick Lane, E1 6QL)
www.vintage-market.co.uk
Twitter: TrumanMarketsE1

The Vintage Market is a subterranean maze of about 100 vintage traders selling all kinds of vintage fashion, jewellery and accessories. The traders here have permanent units where they can store their stock, rather than taking it away at the end of the day and this means that they can hold more stock and also spend more time on their displays. Expect to find neon lights, posters, extravagantly dressed traders and some great background music when visiting this place. It will take a while to explore all the nooks and crannies of this huge basement, but you're bound to come away with a few vintage treasures to add to your collection.

Eat & Drink

There are so many street food stalls on Brick Lane these days that recommending eateries seems unnecessary, but one exception to this is *Beigel Bake* (at the Bethnal Green end of Brick Lane), which is the last of the Jewish eateries in the area and has become something of an institution – open 24 hours a day and serving the best salt beef beigel in town. Next door is *Brick Lane Coffee* which does great cappuccino. Further down, where the railway bridge crosses Brick Lane at number 178, is *Pretty Cuppa*, which is a sweet little place to enjoy coffee and some great cakes.

Visit

If you haven't had enough of markets, there are several great ones in the area. Spitalfields Market (see page 311), Columbia Road (see page 271) and Petticoat Lane (see page 295) are all within walking distance of Brick Lane.

East

Broadway Market

London Fields, E8
www.broadwaymarket.co.uk
Twitter: @Broadway_Mkt
Instagram: broadwaymarket
Overground: London Fields, Cambridge Heath
Open: Saturday 9am-5pm

Joining the crowds at Broadway Market on any Saturday it's difficult
to think that back in 2004, after years of decline, the traditional
street market stopped trading. From this low point the Tenants and
Residents Association and Hackney Council worked to establish an
incredibly diverse market which has gone from strength to strength
in the last 15 years and is now one of east London's major tourist
attractions. It has even spawned several smaller markets in the area
(Netil and Broadway Vegan).

These days over 130 stalls show up here on a Saturday offering all kinds of things from fruit and veg to designer clothing and even one stall specialising in art books. Broadway has lots of great food stalls with several traders selling fine cheeses and salamis and a wide choice of freshly made cakes, pastries and bread. There are a few specialist traders here – one just selling their own brand of chutneys with lots of different flavours and the chance to try before you buy – and another offering their own selection of smoked meats. Carnivores will not be disappointed with several stalls specialising in carefully sourced meat including *Downlands Pork Butchers*. There is a more limited offering of seasonal fruit and veg but the quality is high.

Broadway Market also has lots of designer makers selling anything from handmade kids' wear to bread boards made from recycled wood. There's an excellent haberdashers, *Heza* with their incredibly lovely men's shirts and sweatshirts, and another designer selling stylish bike accessories. The market ends at the junction with Jackman Street, but the best is saved until last, because it is here that Paul's vintage clothing

takes centre stage with lots of rails to sift through and plenty of bargains on the £5 discount rails.

It's sad to note that a few of the old stalwarts of the market, such as the old family butchers and the more basic fruit & veg stall, have left the market, but Broadway is more about shopping for your bits and pieces, finding the odd treat or gift and just enjoying the atmosphere. It is now much closer to the kind of social event of Brick Lane or Greenwich than its origins as a local street market. Visiting the Broadway Market on a sunny Saturday it is heart warming to see so many people enjoying themselves and others doing business. It is now one of London's major markets and well worth making an effort to visit .

Eat & Drink

There are many more street food stalls here these days with many of them congregating at the northern end of the market, making it easier to take your food to sit in London Fields if you feel like it and the weather allows. The Indian food stall just opposite The Cat & Mutton has been here years and does great samosas. For something more traditional there is *F.Cooke* which has been serving pie and mash on this street long before the hipsters arrived.

Visit

Netil Market (see page 291) and Broadway Vegan Market (see page 263) are just around the corner if Broadway hasn't sated your desire to stroll around markets. London Fields is at one end of the market and is a pleasant place to relax in the summer and don't forget to pack your Speedos as there's also a great lido in the park.

Broadway Vegan Market

London Fields Primary School, E8 3RU
Twitter: @BroadwayVeganMK
Instagram: @broadwayveganmarket
www.broadwayveganmarket.com
Open: Saturday 10am-4pm

This latest reincarnation of the Saturday market at London Fields Primary School is timely, with veganism all the rage at the moment. The new market is the brainchild of the people at The Spread, who run a number of markets across London dedicated to food.

Compared to your average market trader, the stall holders here are a cheerful and attractive advertisement for a plant based lifestyle, with lots of samples available and all of them willing to chat about their products and offer advice. Among this hardy band of traders is Sam and Oli from *Natural Born Wine* with a carefully selected range of biodynamic wines and lots of info sheets for those who want to know more. Vegan cheese and nut spreads are available from the wittily named *I Am Nut OK*, while *Nini Organics* offer a range of vegan organic beauty products.

The rest of the market is dedicated to food with delicious vegan cakes provided by the likes of *Lele's Café*, *Cakefully Heaven* and generous helpings of colourful vegan cakes from *Bakings*. For vegan food on the move, you won't be disappointed with vegan Sushi, hearty curries from *Veeg*, Vietnamese vegan food from *Eat Chay* and several stalls offering vegan takes on the traditional burger – among them *The Green Grill*. It's a pity that the market doesn't offer anything in the way of vegan ingredients to prepare your own food, but vegetables are not hard to find and *Abel & Cole* have a stall here promoting their veg box scheme. Let's hope this little plant based market can establish some roots and enjoy some of the success of its neighbours.

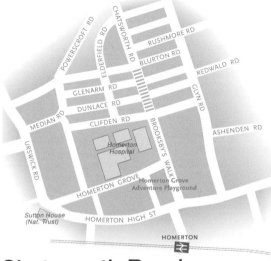

Chatsworth Road

Chatsworth Road (from Clifden Road to Rushmore Road), E5 0LH
www.chatsworthroade5.co.uk
Twitter: @chatsworthroad
Overground: Homerton, Hackney Central, Clapton
Open: Sunday 11am-4pm

Before the war Chatsworth Road Market was one of east London's
biggest with over 200 stalls trading throughout the week. The
proceeding years were not kind to the area or its market and by the
1980s there were just a few stalls left and the market eventually
closed in 1990. Since that time the area has revived and an
enthusiastic local residents and traders association has worked
to revive the shops and introduce a vibrant and diverse Sunday
market which has flourished and become a firm favourite with the
locals and intrepid tourists prepared to venture this far east.
Chatsworth Road is a great place to visit on a Sunday with

delicious street food, vintage clothing and household goods and a wide choice of food stalls allowing visitors to buy a good deal of their weekly shopping on the street. One of the most trusted traders is the fresh fish stall which always has responsibly sourced fresh fish at very reasonable prices. The cheese stall is also a firm favourite offering British and Alpine cheeses with plenty of advice and tasters for the curious. The bakery stall is popular and very well priced and *Downland Produce* is a regular here offering their own organic and free range meat.

Chatsworth Road also has some vintage and new clothing and jewellery with quite a few designers selling their own creations and plenty of discounted items to appeal to committed bargain hunters. The plant and flower stall run by Brett and his family is another favourite, with a great choice of cut flowers and healthy looking plants. He's been trading here for years and even when things are quiet always keeps smiling, 'things will always get better!' And, judging from the changes on Chatsworth Road, he's right.

Street food stalls are well represented, offering treats from around the globe from fresh falafels to good old fashion scotch eggs and sausage rolls. The two lads serving freshly made Tempura Prawns, Kara-age fried chicken and other freshly made Japanese delicacies are very popular and well worth a try.

Chatsworth Road and its market have gone through a transformation in recent years and it's heartening for any market lover to see how, with the support of local residents and traders, a market can rise from the ashes and bring trade and vitality to an area. The situation again changed in late 2017 when Hackney Council assumed sole control of the market. Let's hope they can keep the momentum going and Chatsworth Road can continue to improve.

Chrisp Street

Market Square, Chrisp Street, E14 6AQ
DLR: All Saints
Open: Monday-Saturday 9.30am-4pm (busiest Saturday)
Bombed during the war, the reconstruction of this part of East London was designed by Frederick Gibberd, who also worked on Harlow new town, which this centre still resembles. The market that sets up here pre-dates the post-war architecture and there is still some sense of history and community that transcends the concrete environment. Sadly, the last of the old east end traders, Ken Long, gave up his pitch in the spring of 2018 and so ended a history of trading in fruit and veg that extended back to his great-grandmother, Ellen Walton, who started trading here during the war.

The market continues to cater for the local community and on Saturdays the place is at its busiest with a full complement of about 40 stalls offering a reasonable selection of bargain clothing, fabric and haberdashery, carpets, household goods, shoes, bags and cheap foodstuffs. Despite Ken's departure, there are lots of Asian-run fruit and veg stalls on the market offering an incredible selection of exotic produce like aloo, long kudo and fresh curry leaves. The market has a regular fishmonger selling cheap frozen fish and although there is no meat sold on the market, there are several butchers within the surrounding shopping complex. There have been plans for the redevelopment of Chrisp Street Market for the last 10 years, but these have divided the local community and traders. At present the scheme has been sent back to the local housing association for further consultation.

Columbia Road

Columbia Road east of Ravenscroft Street to Barnet Grove

Shops and a courtyard on Ezra Street E2 7RG

Tube: Old Street, Bethnal Green (then bus)

Rail: Hoxton, Shoreditch High Street

Open: Sunday 8am-2pm

This flower market is easy to find from whichever direction you approach it – just walk in the opposite direction to those weighed down with bedding plants, cut flowers and large potted shrubs. On a busy Sunday morning the streets around the market can often resemble a scene from *Day of the Triffids*, with punters making slow progress as they shamble along, obscured by the massive array of flora they are trying to get home.

Columbia Road Flower Market is a real Sunday institution and has appeal that extends well beyond the green fingered listeners of *Gardeners' Question Time*, with great gift shops, cafés and eateries along the route and the added appeal of two courtyards on Ezra Street offering among other things food and bric-à-brac. Even on the wettest of days there are always a good few hardy buskers providing a musical accompaniment to the whole experience.

The stalls selling cheap cut flowers at the junction with Ravenscroft Street mark the start of the market and always have an enticing selection of flowers at prices well below those of your local florist. Here you can get a huge bouquet for around a tenner and there are plenty of other cut flower stalls along the route, so it's always a good idea to have a shop around before parting with your cash. The cut flowers remain a constant, but the rest of the market varies its stock depending on the season. In the spring it is awash with trays of bedding plants to brighten up a flower box for as little as £4 a tray and lots of larger plants that will give the urban gardener an instant splash of colour. As summer turns to autumn, evergreens begin to dominate with healthy looking shrubs for as little as £4 and plenty of large mature plants such as orange trees (bearing small fruit) for around £20. During the festive season Columbia Road is a great place to come for Christmas trees of all sizes as well as holly, ivy and other yuletide greenery. The market shops also open on selective evenings in the run-up to Christmas for gift shopping, mulled wine and carols.

The central avenue of the market is always a scrum with hundreds of people pushing their way along, often carrying armfuls of plants. If you get tired of the crush, try weaving between the stalls onto the pavement and taking a look at some of the shops that now line the street. There are lots of great gift, furniture, toy and hat shops to check out including the fabulous *Harry Brand* (no.122), and in the middle of the market is *Lee's Sea Food* for a fishy treat. Towards the eastern end of the market are some of the best stalls for herbs with healthy looking pots of thyme, rosemary and sage all for around £1.50 a plant.

Columbia Road Market is not restricted to Columbia Road, but extends onto Ezra Street and the courtyards connected to it. The main courtyard is just off the junction and has several smart shops including *Milagros* selling a great selection of Mexican glassware, tiles and gifts. Further along to the left of the main junction is a courtyard dedicated to second-hand stalls with a good selection of books, clothing and bric-à-brac to sift through, as well as a stall dedicated to French cheese and cold meats and a great coffee stall with lots of accompanying treats. One of the stalwarts of this part of the market is the burly and bearded Shaun, who has been selling a well chosen selection of clothing, pictures, jewellery and objet d'art from here for years. He loves the market but is acutely aware of the changes to the area that have impacted the market:

'Many houses around this market are now selling for well over a million pounds. The well-off arrivals to the area don't use the market in the same way and don't buy market bric-à-brac. The young here, live in shared houses and they don't want to buy my stuff. So it's a hard time for this kind of business.'

But despite the gloomy account of things, Shaun is always cheerful and enjoys talking with passing friends and customers. His stall is one of the joys of Columbia Road.

Columbia Road is one of London's real Sunday treats and a great way to start a mornings market shopping with Brick Lane (see page 249), Spitalfields (see page 311) and Petticoat Lane (see page 295) all within walking distance.

Eat & Drink

If you don't mind eating on the move *Lee's Sea Food* (134 Columbia Road) sells delicious fried calamari and giant prawns with a wedge of lemon and is highly recommended.

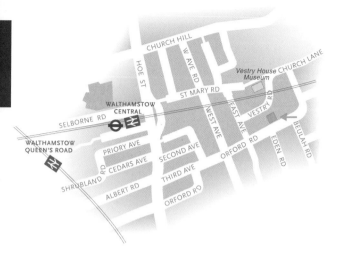

E17 Village Market

Waltham Forest Community Hub, (Asian Centre Building)
18A Orford Road, E17 9LN
Twitter: @E17village
Overground: Walthamstow Central
Rail: Walthamstow Queen's Road
Open: Saturday 10.30am-3.30pm

Walthamstow's E17 Village Market has seen a few management
changes over the last year or so, but is now run by the traders and
for the local community who have taken this friendly little market
to their hearts. One of the organisers is Kostas who runs the very
popular *Greek Café* stall offering delicious hellenic delicacies. He
is joined every Saturday by an excellent indoor plant and cacti stall,
the hot dog stand with the great name 'Walthamstow Dogs', a
carefully chosen and displayed selection of kids' toys and books,
and some good food and drink stalls including the lads offering

delicious Chai tea and one specialising in freshly made Cypriot street food. The offering is completed by a jam stall, locally made fudge and a young couple specialising in delicious low or no carb snacks – all of which offered free tastings.

This is probably one of London's smallest markets, but it is friendly and located on the charming Orford Road, with lots of independent shops, some great cafés and the world famous *God's Own Junkyard*, just around the corner. It is also within ten minutes walk from the massive Walthamstow Market, so you could shop for cheap basics at one of the country's biggest markets and then come here to relax and enjoy a very different vibe.

East

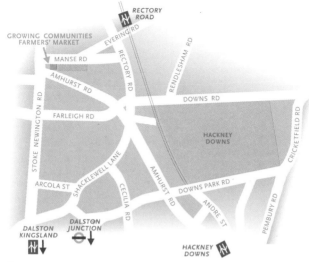

Growing Communities

St Paul's Church Court Yard,
Stoke Newington Road, N16 7UY
www.growingcommunities.org
Twitter: @growcomm
Rail: Rectory Road
Open: Saturday 10am-2.30pm

This market has been supplying organic and locally produced food to the citizens of Hackney since 2003. The market is run by Growing Communities – a Hackney-based social enterprise who promote local farmers and sustainable food production. The organisation also runs a vegetable box scheme supplying produce from its own urban gardens and Dagenham Farm, as well as other local organic farms and makes effort to ensure that the food sold at the market is both locally produced (within about 150 miles from London) and 100% organic.

The application of all these principles might sound a bit worthy and pious, but the market that takes place in the grounds of St Paul's Church, Stoke Newington, is a lot of fun. Over the years the market has acquired a loyal following among the residents of Hackney, who enjoy the food and have got to know and trust the traders. The Saturday market has a really friendly atmosphere and all the stall holders are keen to discuss their produce and explain their work with lots of small-scale farmers including *Sarah Green's Organics* who always make a real effort to display their seasonal produce. Another small holder is *Peach and Pippin* who have a small Essex farm and bring a selection of their fruit and flowers as well as delicious cakes, jams and chutneys, all made from their farm produce. The mushroom stall run by Matt is also a regular here, selling all kinds of cultivated and wild fungi and also preparing delicious mushroom sandwiches from a small gas ring which a very popular. Like all the stallholders here, he is enthusiastic about what he does and is always eager to talk about his produce and dispense advice. One of the jewels in this market's crown is the wonderful *Longwood Organic Farm* stall offering delicious organic beef, pork, lamb and chicken, all reared on their Suffolk farm.

Visitors are spoilt for choice for take-away food with a local Turkish woman making traditional street food using ingredients sourced from the market and plenty of cakes and pastries on hand to satisfy those with a sweet tooth. The organisers have thoughtfully provided a large seating area so people can enjoy their food in comfort and perhaps get a shot of caffeine from the busy coffee stall. Leaving the market after a delicious snack and with a bag full of fresh organic produce, it's not difficult to see why this place has become a permanent and much loved part of Stoke Newington life. The market is just a few minutes walk from Stoke Newington Car Boot Sale which is one of London's best (see page 364).

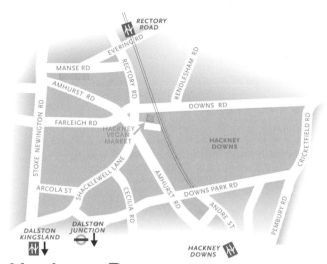

Hackney Downs Vegan Market

Hackney Downs Studios, Amhurst Terrace, E8 2BT
www.fatgayvegan.com
Twitter: @FatGayVegan
Overground: Rectory Road,
Hackney Downs or Hackney Central
Open: Saturday 11am-5pm

Vegan markets seem to be springing up all the time in London – Hackney Downs was the first on the scene and a template for much that has followed. Every Saturday the courtyard of Hackney Downs Studios hosts about 15 vegan street food traders and producers of vegan products.

There's a great choice of street food from around the world with *Bamboo Street Food* offering a fusion of Shawarma Kebab,

Burrito Samosas and Mexican Rice. The Big V London are regulars here and serve some of the best veggie burgers to be found in the capital. Traditional east London fare like pie and mash might not sound like a cuisine readily adaptable to a meat free diet, but there was a stall doing exactly that with plenty of customers willing to pay a tenner for their meal deal. The team at *Eat Chay* offer a great selection of plant-based Vietnamese food such as noodle salad and kimchi fried rice. Despite the queues, they were enthusiastic and happy to chat while they worked about their food's health giving properties.

If you have a sweet tooth there are always a good few specialists offering delicious vegan cupcakes, cookies and pastries. Completing the picture are a few stalls selling vegan scented candles and *Kinda Co.* with a range of non-dairy spreads and deli products to add to any vegans larder and *Clarkshaws Brewery* offering vegan craft beer.

The market is run by Sean O'Callaghan who blogs on all matters vegan under the nom de plume 'Fat Gay Vegan'. He does a good job of promoting the event and alternates stalls so that every week is slightly different from the next. It's a great event and one worth exploring.

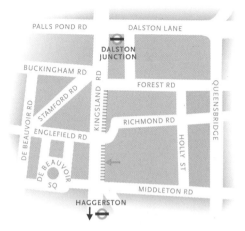

Kingsland Waste

Kingsland Road (Middleton Road to Richmond Road), E8 4AA
Overground: Haggerston
Open: Saturday 10am-2pm

Kingsland Waste has always been a neglected market on the fringes
of Hackney, but somehow it has always survived with its combination
of bric-à-brac, household goods and cheap street fashion appealing to
the low income students and families from the local estates. The last
ten years have been particularly hard on Kingsland Waste and perhaps
the increased gentrification of this part of Hackney has deprived the
market of both its traders and customers. These days there are just
a few stalls and some fly traders who sell junk spread out on the
pavement. There are still some stalwarts that show up here looking for
bargains and the family that run the single extended junk stall always
have some unusual things on offer, but this really is a market hanging
on by the skin of its teeth.

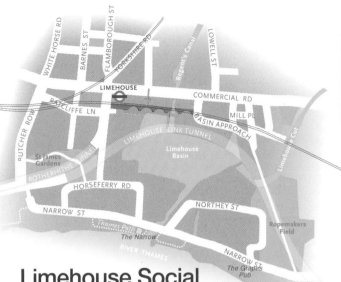

Limehouse Social

Limehouse Basin, next to Limehouse DLR Station, E14 7LB
Twitter: @Limehousebasin
facebook.com/Limehousebasin
Open: Last Saturdays of the month 11am-5pm
(check for additional dates)

Limehouse Basin, with its wide paved avenue, view across the water to moored yachts and sheltered area under the raised DLR, is a perfect place for a little market. When Limehouse Social takes the stage once a month you can expect to find a mix of quality wines, locally sourced honey, freshly made cakes and pastries, some fine deli produce and even a few local start-ups offering naturally produced cosmetics. There are also a good few street food stalls with plenty of sheltered seating to sit and enjoy the food and the view. If your bike needs some attention, there is often a bike man on hand offering reasonably priced repairs.

East

London Fields Sunday Market

London Fields Primary School, Westgate St, London E8 3RL
www.lfsundaymarket.com
Overground: London Fields
Open: Sunday 10am-2pm

This little farmer's market is a regular Sunday fixture with a small group of long-standing traders and loyal customers keeping things going despite a few changes of management over the years. Here you can find great seasonal produce from *Eden Farms* and *Perry Court Farm*. Carnivores can also source quality free range poultry and other meat from *Pastures Farm* and there are plans for a cheese and fishmongers to join the market. *Bread Winners* offer a selection of breads and pastries and there's even a coffee stall if you fancy some caffeine with your carbs. *Bob's Bikes* is a recent addition to the market offering a great selection of bikes and bike parts at very reasonable prices. The market is run with a community spirit and there are regular activities arranged around the market from craft classes to yoga sessions.

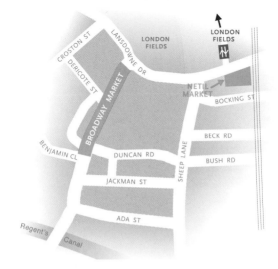

Netil Market

Westgate Street, E8 3RL
www.eatworkart.com/netil-market
Twitter: @netilmarket
Overgound: London Fields
Open: Saturday 11am-6pm

This small walled space just five minutes from Broadway Market (see page 258) has been hosting a Saturday market for quite a while, but in recent years it has become a hub for small independent businesses that occupy permanent trading units and offer anything from smart dog accessories to leather goods, kitchenware and hand-made scented candles. These full-time traders are an important part of the market and several of them also occupy stalls on Saturdays having started as stall holders.

The market is not easy to miss on a Saturday with Terry's collection of second-hand furniture spread along the pavement on Westgate Street as you enter. At the entrance there is a great selection of street food units including *Bao Bar* offering Taiwanese food and *Lemlem Kitchen* for mouthwatering African inspired dishes. Further into the market you can find new camping gear, designer clothing, a stall dedicated to art catalogues and a record stall run by market stalwart James:

> '*I sold books here for years, but gradually interest waned and I started selling a bit of vinyl which was more popular. Now I just sell records and business is pretty good... You need to change to survive these days.*'

Just behind James is Pete's collectables and vintage stall with lots of good deals and a great selection of lamps and clocks. Pete sports a Vietnam Vet look with some aplomb and really enjoys his days on the market particularly when the weather is fine.

The market also boasts an upstairs bar which serves anything from a cold beer to cocktails and is also home to the market's very own Netil Radio (www.netilradio.com), playing music for the relaxed young crowd that have colonised this small square of Hackney.

If you're still in the mood for market shopping, there is also the Broadway Vegan Market (see page 263) and Broadway Market (see page 259) just a few minutes from here.

'I sold books here for years, but gradually interest waned and I started selling a bit of vinyl which was more popular. Now I just sell records and business is pretty good… You need to change to survive these days.'

WATCH PLAY
EAT SHOP

Netil Market
OPEN 11AM - 6PM DAILY
MARKET ON SATURDAYS

East

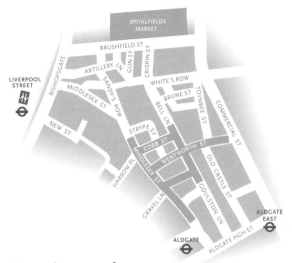

Petticoat Lane

Middlesex Street, Wentworth Street, (and adjacent streets), E1 7JF
Tube: Aldgate (Metropolitan, Circle),
Aldgate East (District, Hammersmith & City), Liverpool Street
(Circle, Central, Hammersmith & City, Metropolitan)
Rail: Liverpool Street
Open: All streets Sunday 9am-2pm,
Wentworth Street only Monday-Friday 10am-2.30pm

Petticoat Lane was renamed Middlesex Street back in 1830, but
the name has stuck largely because this main thoroughfare and
the streets leading from it have remained a place for the sale of
clothing – what used to be called the 'rag trade'. The glass and
steel towers of the city now loom above it but these modest
streets are still home to one of London's most famous street
markets, although now rivalled by Brick Lane (see page 249) and
Spitalfields (see page 311) which are both within walking distance.

Despite the competition, Petticoat Lane is still impressively big and busy on a Sunday, when thousands of people flock to the market from Liverpool Street Station to buy a cheap outfit or just soak up the atmosphere. The streets are lined with hundreds of stalls, concentrating mainly on new clothing, shoes and accessories. Just the sheer amount of people selling shirts or ties is enough to send you into option paralysis. Price-busting multi-packs of knickers, socks and boxer shorts are everywhere, and there is a massive volume of ladies dresses and separates. Although most of the clothing is basic street fashion, there are enough well-made and stylish garments to make a trip here worthwhile. One stall to look out for is the specialist in French Connection seconds and end-of-lines on Wentworth Street, which is popular on a Sunday and is also a feature of Roman Road Market (see page 303) on a Saturday.

In places Petticoat Lane resembles the rag market of Victorian times with stalls selling crumpled nylon clothing in large piles for just £1 and an ever changing flow of the East End's poor sifting through the piles for a bargain. Many of the traders call out for business with one shouting 'So cheap you'll buy it for someone you don't like!' while another just hollered 'cheap, cheap, cheap...' like a demented canary. There is more to the market than just clothing however, with quite a few toy stalls selling cheap and tacky plastic stuff for the kids with the occasional quality item showing up here if you're lucky. As with everything at Petticoat Lane it's a matter of looking around. Petticoat Lane is a good place to find cheap luggage and bags with lots of stalls offering bargains. In addition, there are always one or two decent shoe stalls selling fashionable and cheap footwear for as little as £20 a pair.

Petticoat Lane is also well known for the international textile shops, which sell everything from African wax prints to Indian sari fabric. The prices are very competitive so you can easily afford to do some fairly dramatic curtain-swagging or make yourself a sumptuous dress or skirt. The Middlesex Road end of the market is also a magnet for demonstrators – the people whose job it is to flog us the fragile hope that our lives will be better if we can shred, shine or sharpen something five seconds quicker. Few can resist the power of the patter. *Mr Euro-Tool*, *Mr Shine-Wipe* or *Mr Borner V-Slicer* are performers in the old tradition, so watch, admire and learn. The evangelists at the Liverpool Station end of Middlesex Street might not have such funky props, but the sales message is just as heartfelt: their energetic sing-songs are now a market staple on a Sunday.

Although Sundays is the main day for Petticoat Lane, there is a much smaller weekday market that caters for the locals with a limited selection of clothing, fruit and veg and other staples. The weekday market is a shadow of the Sunday event and only occupies a small part of Wentworth Street.

Eat & Drink

Petticoat Lane Market extends down a number of streets, so there are plenty of places to eat as you go round. *Café le Jardin* (16 Bell Street) might sound fancy but is a long established old school caff, while *Happy Days* on Goulston Street has been serving quality fish and chips for years. If you don't mind eating on the move there are a number of fast food stalls on the market.

Queen's Market

Green Street, South of Upton Park Station,
next to Queen's Road, E13 9BA
Tube: Upton Park (Metropolitan, District)
Open: Tuesday and Thursday-Saturday 9am-5pm

Queen's Market has a long history dating back to Victoria's reign
but in the 1960s the market was moved to this purpose-built
square and in 1979 a low roof was built over it. Despite these
badly-planned changes, it is still thriving and even on a wet
midweek morning crowds mill around the hundred or so stalls in
search of bargains.

One of the reasons this market is still doing well is the large
Asian and African communities in Upton Park who still prefer the
hustle and bustle of a market to the antiseptic atmosphere of a
supermarket. The market is great value for fruit and veg with lots
of stalls competing for your custom and plenty of bargains if you

are prepared to shop around. Eddie has been running his grocery stall at the front of the market for years, having started trading here over 45 years ago. His main complaint is with the council and their parking:

> *'People don't have money around here and the council have put paid parking all round the market. £2 an hour might not sound a lot to some, but it's putting off some customers who want to use the car to do a big shop. We complain but they don't listen.'*

Queen's is also a great place to find Asian and African produce, with many specialist food outlets offering things like dasheen leaves and bunches of fresh pak choi. The handful of fresh fish stalls have a varied range of catches and are good value with staples like smoked haddock alongside more exotic things like conger eel and octopus. In addition there are several butchers on site offering all manner of bloody bargains as well as a stall selling farm-fresh eggs.

Queen's Market is a good place for cheap fabric with many stalls offering colourful and plain material (including African and Asian designs) with prices starting from £1 per metre. If sewing isn't your thing, there are stalls selling cheap and cheerful clothing and bargain footwear. Although some of the consumer durables are of limited appeal, there are always good bargains to be found: one trader offers quality white crockery for just £2 a plate and a choice of stainless steel pans at below shop prices.

Queen's Market is a place where everything is cheap and people count every penny. It would take a strong person to carry £20 of groceries back from here and if you're a bargain hunter this place is definitely worth making the journey to visit for a week's shop. Saved from the threat of redevelopment, this market seems destined to survive for decades to come.

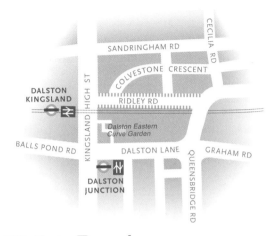

Ridley Road

Ridley Road, between Kingsland High Street
and St Mark's Rise, E8 2NP
Rail: Dalston Kingsland, Hackney Downs
Open: Monday-Saturday 9am-5pm

Ridley Road is one of East London's biggest markets, with attitude
to match. Running the length of a street of lock-up shop units
between Kingsland High Street and St Mark's Rise, this market
is the place where locals from Dalston's diverse communities
come to stock up on cheap food and essentials. The market used
to be very busy throughout the week but there are signs that the
gentrification of Dalston is taking its toll on the market as young
professionals move into the area and choose to do their shopping
elsewhere. Ridley Road is still very busy at the Kingsland Road
junction, but towards St Mark's Rise things are a lot quieter and
there are several gaps in the formerly regimented stalls.

The Afro-Caribbean influence in both Dalston and its market is still strong, and not only in terms of the massive selection of unusual food products. As the crowds of people increase towards midday, the lively – and occasionally slightly abrasive – atmosphere is stoked by shops blasting out reggae and groups of traders and shoppers stopping mid-flow to shoot the breeze.

Although Ridley Road is by no means just a food market, the extensive selection of both fresh and preserved produce is probably the magnet drawing most shoppers. Further down towards St Mark's Rise goods become increasingly diverse, with tropical standards like mango, cassava and sweet potato joined by baskets and trestles piled with unfamiliar leaves, vegetables, meat and fish, and lurid drinks like 'Sky Juice' on sale by the glass. The sheer number of rival stalls and shops means you are spoilt for bargains, with each trader offering something at a discount. Ridley Road is a great place to get a week's fresh produce for under £20 and many visitors leave the market weighed down with more shopping than they should sensibly carry. Staples like lentils, oil, nuts and flour are all very cheap but sold in large bags that make a strong back, or trolley, essential.

In addition, the substantial local Turkish community means that there are plenty of Mediterranean vegetables on offer, with good prices on key ingredients like lemons and flat-leaf parsley. There is also a huge Turkish food shop on the junction with St Mark's Rise that is ideal for all the other Mediterranean foodstuffs you can't find on the market. Most street markets these days do not have a fish stall; Ridley Road has several, selling anything from British stalwarts like cod and haddock, to more exotic species like red snapper and huge conger eels. At one fish stall the crabs were still struggling in vain to escape their fate.

The squeamish will also find Ridley Road difficult to cope with as it is peppered with stalls selling meat and fish products which bear little resemblance to the innocuous vacuum-packed portions in Tesco's: turkey gizzards, saltfish, goat stomachs, cows' and pigs' feet are all piled up, picked over and chopped up in full view.

Food is definitely the thing at Ridley Road, but there are plenty of other goods on offer, with standard market clobber (electricals, cheap and brand-name clothes and shoes, bedding, underwear, cosmetics and hair accessories) dotted throughout, and a smattering of textile units and stalls selling haberdashery and vivid materials like African wax prints, sequined voiles and rainbow selections of satin, cotton and acrylic mixes.

The market might be facing hard times, but a quiet day on Dalston Market is still a pretty busy and interesting experience. With so many week day markets changing into places to eat street food, Ridley Road is now one of the last of a dying breed, let's hope the new arrivals to the area begin to appreciate what's on their doorstep.

Eat & Drink

The *Almond Lane Coffee House*, at the St Mark's Rise end of the market, is one of the few places to get a coffee and a snack on the main strip. For something more substantial there's *Shangai* at 41 Kingsland Road, that serves dim sum throughout the day in a listed interior that used to belong to a traditional pie and mash shop.

Visit

The Rio Cinema is just a short walk up Kingsland Road and is a rare example of an Art Deco cinema. Further along on a Saturday is Stoke Newington Car Boot Sale (see page 366) which is one of the best in the capital.

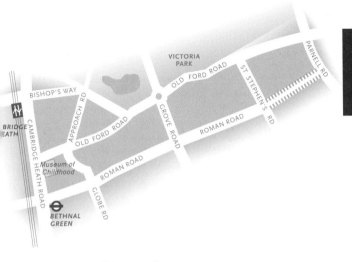

Roman Road

Roman Road from St Stephen's Road to Parnell Road, E3 5EU
Tube: Bow Road (District, Hammersmith & City)
Mile End (Central, District, Hammersmith & City)
Rail: Bow Church DLR
Open: Tuesday, Thursday and Saturday 8.30am-4.30pm

Roman Road and its market are a strange mix of the cosmopolitan
and the parochial. Approaching the market along Roman Road you
will pass a photography gallery, an art gallery and even a Buddhist
Centre, and yet by the time you reach the market it feels as though
you are in the heart of the East End. Most of the people who shop
here are locals and one of the stall-holders spoke of the other side of
Victoria Park as though it were some distant and exotic land. This
end of Roman Road seems relatively untouched by gentrification, but
the market itself is a surprisingly friendly and pleasant place to shop
and one of the best markets to find discounted High Street fashion.

The mysterious stall that sells women's garments one at a time from a box is still going strong. The pitch is always surrounded with eager local women waiting for the next item in the hope that it will be in a style they like and in a size that fits them – price is never a problem as most items are sold for just a few pounds. There are other more conventional clothing stalls along this part of the market and one trader at the centre of the market always has a great selection of French Connection seconds and surplus stock for a fraction of the usual price. There are several shoe stalls offering a selection of fashionable footwear with prices starting from around £20 a pair and this is also a good market to find bargain bags and suitcases, bedding and even a modest flower stall offering bedding plants and cut flowers.

Roman Road Market is still a great place to spend a morning, but it's been affected by big shopping centres like Westfield in Stratford and the council's introduction of parking restrictions in the surrounding area. Whichever way you come here, it's worth the journey – you're bound to leave with a few bargains and a smile on your face.

Eat & Drink

Cafe Creme on the corner of Gladstone Place serves a good cappuccino as does *Mono London* (just opposite Ewart Place) which is one of the few places with outdoor seating. If you fancy some traditional Cockney fare you could try the eel, pie and mash shop, *G. Kelly* or walk to the *Saucy Kipper* at 626 Roman Road for a fish and chip take-away supper.

Visit

The *Idea Store* situated on Gladstone Place, just off Roman Road, is a fantastic new type of library. It offers internet access as well as books and even has a coffee shop. On fine days it's well worth making the journey down St Stephen's Road to explore the Grand Union Canal and Victoria Park.

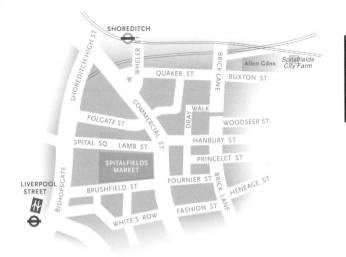

Spitalfields

16 Horner Square, London E1 6EW

www.oldspitalfieldsmarket.com

Twitter: @oldspitalfields or @spitalfieldse1

Tube/Rail: Liverpool Street (Central, Metropolitan, Hammersmith & City)

Open: Daily 10am-5pm (crafts market)

Thursday 8am-3pm (antiques and collectables and a Crafts market)

First and Third Friday of month (Vinyl Market)

For nearly a century Spitalfields was a rough-and-ready fruit and veg wholesale market. The wholesale operation moved to new industrial premises to the east in the early 1990s and the old building has been adapted into a gift and tourist market to rival nearby Brick Lane. The market and shopping complex that exists today is very different from its early beginnings and while the

Victorian wrought iron structure remains intact, much else has been transformed over the last thirty years. Spitalfields is now an upmarket shopping area with smart restaurants, expensive boutiques and, towards the Liverpool Street end of the market, an imposing Norman Foster-designed glass office block that takes centre stage and is the head office of a major bank.

The market has continued despite all the upheaval and quite a few of the old stall holders – including Tom, who sells a fine selection of men's retro shirts – are still going strong. The booksellers continue to be an important part of the market, offering good quality fiction for just a few quid. The market has its fair share of interesting bric-à-brac stalls with one trader turning his table into an elaborate edifice of antique rugs, pictures and mirrors. There are a few bargains to be found at the market despite the smart environment, with one trader selling all trousers for £10 and dresses and jackets for only £20 and several of vintage sellers offering discount rails for determined bargain hunters.

Further through the market, as the building becomes more modern, the stalls change with the emphasis shifting to new goods and plenty of stalls offering independent designer clothing and accessories. Here you can find a funky selection of hand-made jewellery and stylish women's fashion is particularly well represented with many London designers selling their wares . Men don't have as much choice but there are still some interesting things to find here including one trader selling fabulous Seamus Jones shirts made from Liberty prints for £55. Not all the clothes on sale at the market are hand-made and original designs, but even the imported, unbranded gear is of good quality. Here you can find cheap but fashionable rucksacks for under £20, a great choice of original T-shirts for around £15 and the gadget stall is a regular here offering all kinds of unusual electronic novelty gifts at below high street prices.

Some old school market lovers might miss the rough-and-ready nature of Spitalfields in its early days, but it's clear that this new environment is popular, with a busy market of some nature taking place throughout the week, including a regular (first and third Friday) vinyl market – for those audiophiles who are still wedded to their hi-fi systems and the magic of the long-playing record.

The particular make-up of the market will change from day to day, but street food has definitely taken hold here with a large food court offering great value and delicious street food at competitive prices. There's even a dedicated seating area making this a great place to relax with some food and inspect your latest purchases.

The Antiques & Collectables Market
Open: Thursday 8am-5pm

About 60 stalls show up here every Thursday selling anything from bric-à-brac and retro clothing to collectables and fine antiques. Spitalfields has kept enough of its old character to make it an ideal setting for such a market and although more space is now being allocated for street food, it is still the largest antiques market in London, closely followed by Covent Garden on Mondays and Bermondsey on a Friday. Antiques and collectables is a pretty broad term and among the stalls there are all kinds of things from second-hand books to recently discarded toys, paintings of all ages and varying quality, reproduction object d'art and also some genuine and valuable antiques. The stall selling an odd assortment of old photos and bowler hats is fascinating and well worth a browse. The antique and used jewellery stalls are also popular here with young tourists always eager to paw through the piles of discarded trinkets in the hope of finding a treasure. Vintage fashion is also well represented with lots of London's young and trendy taking time out to trawl through the rails for something unique to add to their wardrobe. And there are always a few discounted rails where the occasional bargain can be found.

Many of the traders are eclectic in what they sell and their stalls are always fun to explore, but there are also collectors here that specialise and are knowledgeable in their subject. One such stall is run by Mark Motty who has a remarkable collection of vintage prescription and sun glasses and trades as *Dr. Retrospex*. He seems to enjoy his work and is able to talk with enthusiasm about his collection and some of the rare specs that he keeps under lock and key and only shows on request. Another specialist trader is Ray Walters who deals in vintage and modern pens and takes great care with the display of his beautiful writing instruments.

The antiques and collectables market runs parallel the arts and craft market. So as you walk through the building towards Liverpool street you will find about 30 more stalls selling new clothing and accessories that are here throughout the week.

Eat & Drink

There are all kinds of eateries and cafés within Spitalfields these days, so visitors are spoilt for choice with the chance to eat your way around the globe from Indian curries to Korean BBQ. If you fancy escaping the market, Brick Lane, and its famous Indian restaurants, is just five minutes east of here.

Visit

Spitalfields is within walking distance of several great markets with Brick Lane (see page 249) to the east and Petticoat Lane just a little way along Commercial Road (see page 295). If you've had enough of markets, Denis Severs House (www. dennissevershouse.co.uk) is not far from here at 18 Folgate Street and offers a quirky look at the history of Spitalfields Huguenot silk weavers.

Victoria Park

Night Walk (between Bonner Gate and Gore Gate)
Victoria Park, E2 9JW
www.victoriaparkmarket.com
Twitter: @VictoriaParkMk
Tube: Bethnal Green (Central)
Open: Sunday 10am-4pm

This food market is a new arrival on the London scene, but is run by the experienced team behind Putney Market and takes place in the fantastic Victoria Park. The success of this kind of high quality food market really depends upon the local community, and the good folk of Hackney seem to have taken this event to their hearts with such a good turn out in the first few months that the opening times have been extended.

What draws the local punters is the great atmosphere and excellent food with organic fruit and veg, fresh quality breads and cakes, a good butchers and *The Fresh Fish Shop* selling all kinds of seasonal produce from a small dinghy. There are also several cheese merchants giving visitors a good choice of British and continental varieties. There are plenty of moreish deli ingredients such as olives, fresh pasta and a popular trader specialising in their own unique mushroom paté – with plenty of samples to allow you to try before you buy.

Not all the visitors to the market want to buy groceries and towards Bonner Gate there are a few street food stalls offering food from around the globe and a good ice cream stall for something sweet. The market organisers have also thoughtfully provided seating so you can enjoy your meal in comfort. In addition there is a quality beer stall for those who fancy an early pint. The market's location in Victoria Park is ideal for the dog deli stall that has all kinds of treats for your four-legged friend.

Victoria Park Market is a lot of fun and also really useful for the kind of clientele that now live around the park. Gentrification might be a bad thing for markets like Bethnal Green and East Street, but in this case it appears the making of this great little market!

Walthamstow

Walthamstow High Street, E17 7LD
Tube/Rail: Walthamstow Central (Victoria)
Rail: St James Street
Open: Monday-Saturday 9am-5pm

Many locals claim that this is the longest market in Britain,
which is probably an exaggeration given the size of Portobello
Market (see page 141), but it is certainly quite a trek from St
James Street to the end of the market at Hoe Street. Many local
markets are now facing difficulties, but Walthamstow is a rare and
wonderful exception. There are many reasons for Walthamstow's
continued success, among them the pedestrianisation of the wide
thoroughfare of Walthamstow High Street, making it a great place
for shopping and strolling. The shops in the area complement the
market rather than compete with it, with some excellent butchers,
fishmongers and continental food retailers.

There are about 500 stalls lining the half mile route of the market selling all kinds of merchandise from groceries to kitchenware and kids' toys. Although the clothing is not as trendy as that found at Camden Market, there are plenty of stalls selling street fashion at keen prices, including overstocks and slight seconds from High Street brands like River Island, Monsoon and M&S for £5 a garment. Among the many fabric stalls on the market, there's a particularly good one on the junction with Palmerston Road, offering quality curtain fabric for as little as £3.99 per metre. Another stall, further along, sells Asian and African fabrics at very low prices. Kitchenware and household goods are widely available too, with anything from large aluminium pans to kitchen roll at well below shop prices.

Walthamstow is also a great place to get fresh fruit and veg with lots of stalls competing for business and plenty of discounted bulk offers like a box of plum tomatoes for just £3 and three bunches of coriander for only £1. There are lots of fishmongers along the strip, all of them offering great value and a wide choice of fishy fare.

Unusual stalls at Walthamstow Market include the CD stall which offers a massive selection of music for just a few quid. CDs are becoming a thing of the past, but some people have them in their car and for a few quid they can add to their in-car music collection. The market also has two stalls where the name of Dyson is mud, trading as they do in Hoover bags and accessories. For romantics who would rather return to their loved one with flowers than vacuum cleaner accessories, there are several stalls selling cut flowers and one dealing in cheap bedding plants. Among the good deals were large pots of heather for just a few quid a pot. Another unusual feature of the market is the stall specialising in leather goods run by a friendly Polish man, who is happy to repair items and add the occasional hole to his range of great value leather belts.

Walthamstow High Street is an ideal place to visit if you want to see a neighbourhood market still in its prime. Unlike many local markets it's busy even on a weekday – although Saturday is the best day to go. A good way to approach the market is through the wonderful Springfield Park and Walthamstow Nature Reserve, which will take about 45 minutes, but gives you a soothing dose of nature before the hustle and bustle of the market. At the other end of the market you are about ten minutes from Walthamstow Village and its Saturday market (see page 321) which is a more gentle market experience and a relaxing way to round off an afternoon shop.

Eat & Drink

Among the best places to find good British food on the market is *Copperfield Snack Bar* (at the top end near Hoe Street), as well as *Bunters' Grill* and *First Stop Cafe* (in the middle part of the market). *L.Manze* pie and mash shop is an established favourite, while *Cafe Rio* is a more recent, but equally popular café with seating outside on fine days. If you don't mind eating on the move there are lots of food stalls on the market including *Seth's Spice Hut* for Indian snacks.

Visit

Walthamstow High Street has some interesting shops along its route with many charity shops including the largest Oxfam shop in the capital at the Blackhorse Road end of the market. There is also a great range of fabric shops on the High Street and some excellent food shops which, combined with the market, make this a great place to shop on a weekend.

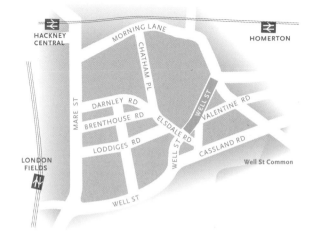

Well Street

Well Street, E9 6QU
www.wellstreetmarket.co.uk
Twitter: @WellStShopping
Instagram: @wellstreetshopping
Rail: Homerton, Hackney Central
Open: First Saturday of the month 10am-4pm

In October 2008 Martin Wiles, the last permanent trader on Well Street, set up his fruit and veg stall for the last time, ending his family's 50 years of trading on the street and marking the end of a market that had been going since 1862. At that time it appeared that the market's days were over, but with the help of some enthusiastic locals and traders, the support of the council and a successful crowdfunding campaign; the market relaunched in the winter of 2016 as a monthly event.

About 20 stalls set up here offering delicious breads and pastries, organic meat, hand-made jewellery from local designers and a few traders offering vintage clothing and bric-à-brac. The organisers also aim to involve local youngsters and there are lots of opportunities for startup businesses to get involved, as well as regular activities such as face painting and live music to accompany the shopping. The market is a lot of fun and there are a few street food stalls if you want to eat on the go, as well as great cafés including *Well Street Kitchen* and *The Grand Howl*.

Following a change in policy, the market is again under the sole management of Hackney Council. Let's hope this change in organisation can maintain some of the enthusiasm and energy that witnessed the market's revival in recent years.

East

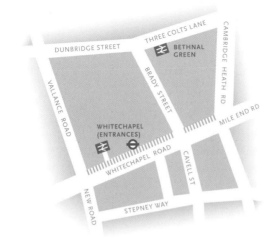

Whitechapel Market

North side of Whitechapel Road, from Vallance Road to
Cambridge Heath Road, E1 1BY
Tube/Overground: Whitechapel (District, Hammersmith & City)
Open: Monday-Saturday 8.30am-5.30pm,
Thursday 8.30am-1pm

Whitechapel has a long history as a place of immigration and
its High Street has been the site of street trading since the 17th
century. The market and its immigrant population have been
intimately connected for centuries, and where once Jewish and
Irish traders sold their wares, now it is the local Bengali, Punjabi
and Bangladeshi community that predominate and make this one
of London's few thriving weekday markets.

Whitechapel has always been a home to the poor and
although the prosperity of the City is now encroaching on the
area, the market is still a place where price and value for money

are paramount. The fabric stalls are all very cheap with plenty of unusual designs and patterns to choose from. The clothing and shoe stalls offer generic street fashion at very low prices and there is even a stall specialising in remainder shoes for just a few quid a pair. The most unusual traders are the two fish men who both sell huge frozen fish from large freezers placed on the pavement. The fish are packaged and bear names such as *Rohn* and *Bual* and do not look appetising for those unfamiliar with them. It might be better to stick to the fresh mackerel and haddock which are also available.

Whitechapel also has stalls selling small electrical goods, haberdashery, bags, kids' clothes and toys, and a trader selling good value kitchen equipment; but the market really excels when it comes to fresh fruit and veg. There is a wealth of choice to be found here extending from the basics to more exotic things like fresh curry leaves and bitter gourd. This is a great place to do your weekly shop on a budget with big bags of onions for just £1.50 and a bag of coriander for just £1.

Whitechapel Market is a place were all kinds of cultures and races mix and where London's diversity is displayed in all its complexity. At one stall a burly turban-wearing Sikh trader talks to a friend in the broadest cockney accent while at another stall a Bangladeshi trader could speak hardly any English and seemed an exotic import from another world. These people are carrying on a market tradition that has deep roots in London's history and when so many weekday markets are declining or becoming venues for street food, Whitechapel is a wonderful throwback and one to be treasured.

Eat & Drink

Whitechapel High Street does have a few rather dodgy pubs, but is poorly served for cafés and restaurants. *Peckish?* (no.315) is a small sandwich bar which does a reasonable coffee. The *Mouse Tail Café* (at no.307) does great coffee and has seating where you can watch the world go by. For Indian food it might be better to try some of the places on Brick Lane – just ten minutes walk from the market.

Visit

The main cultural landmark in this part of town is the Whitechapel Art Gallery which displays modern art and has the added appeal of a great coffee shop. The *Idea Store* is a new kind of library at the eastern end of the market, which is a popular resource for the local population and is well worth a visit.

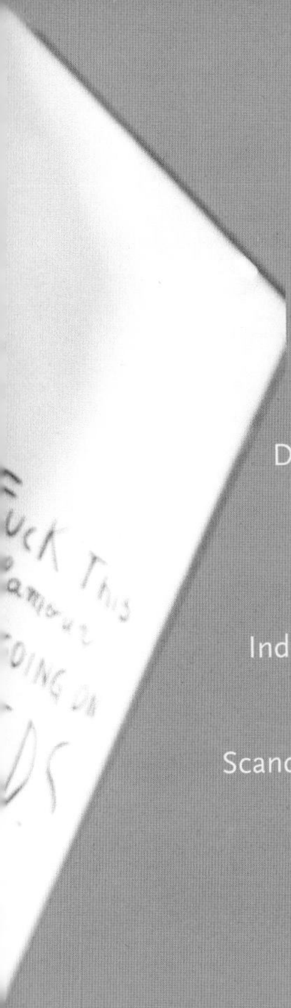

POP UP MARKETS

Classic Car Boot Sale

Various London locations
www.classiccarbootsale.co.uk
Twitter: @classiccarboot
Instagram: classiccarboot

This wonderful event manages to combine just about every aspect of vintage life in one venue including retro clothing of all kinds, collectable household goods and vinyl, beautiful film cameras and of course some great classic cars, bikes and motorbikes. Wayne Hemingway, the designer who formerly ran *Read or Dead*, is the man behind the event where people sell their vintage stuff from vintage cars and with his dedicated team has made this wacky idea a reality. Mr Hemingway has not just put his name to the event but is clearly involved and can be seen wondering among the stalls and chatting with visitors and traders.

Although not everyone has a classic car at their disposal there are enough here to keep petrol heads happy. Commitment to the wearing of vintage gear is likewise variable but there are enough people sporting a stylish retro look to keep people watchers happy. It is also great to see so many visitors getting involved and coming in full outfit and no doubt hoping to add to their collection.

The atmosphere is unlike any other car boot you'll visit with the emphasis on retro style and glamour rather than the usual wandering around a windy field looking at clobber. There is always a DJ playing suitably classic soul, pop and Motown and some great food stalls if all the people, cars, bikes, cameras and clothes makes you peckish.

The Classic Car Boot Sale takes place in London about twice a year, but this makes it all the more special. Check out their website for forthcoming events and get your vintage glad rags on, you're guaranteed to have a ball.

Crafty Fox Market

www.craftyfoxmarket.co.uk
www.shoppingwithsoul.co.uk
Twitter/Instagram: @craftyfoxmarket

Crafty Fox Markets started back in 2010 when Sinead Koehler, who had been selling jewellery at various markets around London, decided to start her own event which would act as a supportive hub for traders. The markets she started under the name Crafty Fox have gone from strength to strength by offering organised, well publicised events where traders get a fair deal.

Their regular events usually involve additional activities such as craft workshops with both adults and children engrossed in the process of cutting, gluing and painting their creations. The shopping experience is of course the main event, with at least 30 stalls displaying hand-made crockery, cards, unique jewellery, framed pictures and accessories. The traders are well chosen with some particularly high-quality independent jewellers, offering end-of-season discounts. *Jill* (shopjill.com) is a regular here selling her bird/bunny inspired designs on purses, bags and even framed. She loves the Crafty Fox markets:

'A lot of effort is put into the markets and they are always well attended. As a stall holder you always feel they want you to do well. Their markets are are also really friendly.'

The ceramicist trading as *Stolen Form* (stolenform.com) is also a regular here, offering all kinds unusual and witty ceramics such as brick shaped vases and small bowls in the form of plumbing pipe fittings. He, like many other traders, also had plenty of samples and end-of-lines on offer at a discount, making these events great for bargain hunters.

Crafty Fox host regular markets at venues in south and east London and are well worth seeking out. Take a look at their website for details of future events.

Crafty North Londoner

www.craftynorthlondoner.com
Twitter: @Craftynolo
Instagram: @craftynolo

This local pop-up craft market brings the designer-makers of Haringey, Hackney and Islington to a venue somewhere in north London. Expect to find a classy mix of about 30 traders offering unique jewellery, artwork, natural cosmetics, ceramics, lighting and textiles. The events are well run, with an in-house café, and entry is free. Take a look at their website or social media to find out about forthcoming events

Crafty Fox Market

DIY Art Market

www.diyartmarket.com
Twitter / Instagram: @diyartmarket
Occasional events at locations in Hackney and Peckham

If you want proof that London is a city packed with young creative people, you could do a lot worse than attend one of these DIY Art Markets where a vast number of painters, cartoonists, fanzine publishers, printmakers, jewellers and textile artists congregate to display and sell their wares.

At any of these events you're bound to encounter work that is original, sometimes beautiful, but very often thought provoking and downright funny. The events are full of the kind of youthful enthusiasm that is great to experience. I loved the ceramic plates with erotic depictions in a kind of primitive style and the radical fanzines with all kinds of leftfield political ideas and images. One stall represented an Eastern European art collective with a really unusual collection of print designs that seemed a modern take on the old Soviet-style posters. There are so many great things here if you like contemporary art and design that you are bound to find something to take away and treasure. I am still chuckling at the handful of funny cloth badges I bought from a young artists calling herself *J W Badges* and the A2 photographic poster I bought is still looking for a frame but will no doubt find its place on our office wall.

These markets are really great places to visit just for the fun of it and a lot of the artists seem to be here as much for the fun of it as to do business. One T-shirt on display by artist Babak Ganjei declared 'ART IS THE THING NOBODY ASKED YOU TO DO' and that seems to embody the spirit of the event and, although nobody asked, I'm glad this group of over 80 creatives are doing their thing.

Duck Pond Market Highgate

Lauderdale House, Highgate Hill, N6 5HG
www.duckpondmarket.com
Twitter / Instagram: @duckpondmarket
Tube: Archway (Northern Line)
Open: Second Sunday in March, June, September and December
11am-5pm

This quarterly arts and crafts market is held in the wonderful
16th century Lauderdale House, in the grounds of Waterlow Park.
Regardless of the season you can expect to find an interesting mix
of textiles, ceramics, clothing, accessories, original artwork and a
few artisanal food producers. The occasional nature of the event
helps keep it special and the Duck Pond team always make an
effort with extra activities like face painting and live music. Take a
look at their website for information about the next market.

E17 Designers

www.e17designers.co.uk
Twitter: @E17Designers
Instagram: E17designers
Regular events at venues across Walthamstow

E17 Designers markets take place at a number of venues across
Walthamstow, but the lack of a permanent location and varied
dates only seems to add to their appeal. The market's success
is largely due to the enthusiasm and energy of the organisers,
who make an effort to promote each season's markets and over
a decade of trading have acquired a great reputation and a loyal
following. Each market draws about 25-30 designer-makers
offering jewellery, stylish knit wear, handmade clothing for
adults and their offspring, artwork and original textiles as well as
accessories and homewares. The stalls are almost all staffed by

the designer-makers, who are keen to talk about their wares and how they are made.

The atmosphere at these events is very upbeat with lots of regulars showing up to chat and shop and few leaving without a bag of goodies and a smile. The events are more than just a place to shop with occasional workshops, craft or facepainting for children and live music or DJ performances all part of the show and free entry to boot. Take a look at their website or follow on social media to find out about forthcoming events.

E17 Designers

Hackney Flea Market

Abney Hall, 73A Stoke Newington Church Street, N16 0AY
www.hackneyfleamarket.com
Twitter: @HackneyFlea
Open: Saturday & Sunday 11am-6pm (once a month)

The Hackney Flea has acquired a great reputation and this attracts around 40 traders offering anything from vintage gardening tools to new designer jewellery to this small but quaint hall in the heart of Stoke Newington.

Annie is a regular here with her vintage copper pans starting from £60 and a great selection of vintage posters. She loves the market and her stuff has proved popular with the young stokie crowd. A few stalls further along is Charleen offering a carefully chosen selection of vintage jewellery and accessories. There's lots of vintage clothing stalls to accompany the jewellery with anything from used NB trainers for twenty quid to authentic 1950s dresses.

The atmosphere at the Hackney Flea is always friendly and perhaps because it only takes place one weekend a month there's a real buzz to the event. The tea and cake stall here is also incredibly good with plenty of freshly baked treats to reward you after a hard mornings pottering.

Hackney Record Fair

www.hackneyfleamarket.com
Twitter: @HackneyFlea

This occasional event is perfect for those wedded to their turntables and looking to add to their vinyl collection. Among the traders are record stores, indi labels and a fair few dealers, all offering crate upon crate to sift through in search of vintage gold. DJ's play throughout the day and there's a café for when the going gets tough. Take a look at their website for future events.

Hackney Flea Market

Local Makers Market

Independent Ceramics Market

Independent Ceramics Market

Hoe Street Market

Walthamstow Trades Hall and front carpark
(Next to Yard Sale Pizza), E17 4QR
Facebook: HoeStMarket
Twitter: @hoestmarket
Instagram: hoestmarket
Tube/Rail: Walthamstow Central (7 minute walk or bus)
6 times a year (usually on the second Sunday of the month)

This small market takes place at the furthest end of the very
long Hoe Street, near to Forest Road, so very much a local event
appealing to passing citizens of E17. It is run with enthusiasm by
Kate and brings together some of Walthamstow's most interesting
artists, artisans and designers, offering a selection of quality
artwork, ceramics, cacti and houseplants and original textiles for
the home. There are hot food stalls in the front car park on Hoe
Street and you can take food inside where there is a cheap bar.
Check their social media to find out about forthcoming events.

Independent Ceramics Market

www.hackneyfleamarket.com
Twitter: @HackneyFlea
Instagram: diyartmarket

Run by the Hackney Flea team that also bring you the DIY Art
Market, this event puts London's ceramicists and DIY potters
centre stage. There are plenty of new young ceramic artists
showing their work who are exhibiting alongside established
ceramicists from various London studios including Turning
Earth, Glebe Road and Peckham Kiln Rooms. There really is
something for everyone here, from a delicate vase in muted
colours with a matt glaze to a huge brightly coloured dish

depicting a bacchanalian scene that should definitely be put away when the vicar comes for tea. The prices are very reasonable with lots of things for around the £30 mark and plenty of little ceramic things for just a few quid. Take a look at their website for forthcoming events.

Local Makers Market

www.localmakers.uk
Twitter: @LocalMakers_
Instagram: localmakersmarket
Regular events from April to December

Local Makers is fairly new to the London market scene and are a welcome addition with their enthusiasm and energy. The markets started in Wanstead, but have now expanded to other venues in east London, including Hackney Wick and Stoke Newington. The location may vary but the quality of the traders is always very high with genuine artisan designers offering unique clothes, framed original prints and cards, handmade jewellery and accessories, craft beer, naturally made toiletries and, of course, more succulents than you can point a cactus at! The markets take place from the spring until Christmas and are always well publicised on their website and through social media.

It's great to visit a market run with such generosity with no entry fee and a great little vegan pop-up café offering all kinds of homemade treats. Check out their website for details of the forthcoming events – they are definitely worth making a special effort to visit.

Peckham Salvage Yard

Copeland Gallery, 133 Copeland Road, SE15 3SN
Rail: Peckham Rye, Queen's Road Peckham
www.hackneyfleamarket.com
Twitter: @hackneyflea
Instagram: hackneyfleamarket
Open: 11-6pm on occasional weekends (see website for details)

This regular event is the largest vintage market in south London and much loved by the good people of Peckham who flock here for collectable home wares, vintage clothing and curiosities. One of the market's great attractions is the location just opposite Peckham Rye station, amid a complex of old industrial buildings that once housed a cricket bat factory, but now serves as a social hub with bars, live music venues, a cinema and several interesting independent businesses including *SeaBass Cycles*.

On market days you will find about 70 traders offering a great selection of vintage and nearly-new clothing, 20th Century furniture, ceramics and glass ware from the practical to the collectable, antique luggage, vinyl, old and reproduction posters, as well as the occasional oddity such as the large plastic deer head that took pride of place on a recent visit. One interesting stall holder specialises in vintage wooden radios which have kept their classic looks, but are updated with digital radio and wi-fi. The market is organised by the same people that run Hackney Flea Market, so many of the great stalls you can find at their other events in Stoke Newington and Dalston also trade here.

Peckham Salvage Yard takes place on occasional weekends, but this makes it feel like a special event and always ensures a great atmosphere and lots of visitors. The closest place to relax with a drink is *The Nines* just outside the yard, but there are quite a few eateries in the Bussey Building just around the corner.

Pop up Markets

Scandinavian Market

Albion Street, Rotherhithe, SE16 7HZ
www.scandimarket.co.uk
Twitter/Instagram: @scandimarket
Bi-annual event in the Spring and run-up to Christmas

It might seem strange that a bi-annual Scandinavian Market is held in a quiet back street of Rotherhithe, but the area has a long association with the Scandinavian community who settled here having worked at nearby Surrey Quays. Albion Street is still the home to both the Finnish and Norwegian Churches which jointly run the market.

The Scandinavians certainly seem to have the edge on the Brits when it comes to winter festivities and the Christmas Market that takes over Albion Street in the run-up to Christmas is an incredible event extending over three days and involving over fifty stalls. The Danish have captured the imagination with the concept of Hygge, which might best be translated as the pleasure gained from winter cosiness and this market has a good deal of Hygge to go around.

There are chunky Norwegian wooly gloves, colourful Danish dishcloths and, to create the right ambience, hand-made Swedish candles. Wherever you look there are chunky jumpers, beautifully made scarves and more comfy slippers than you can wave a stick at. The large marquee in the centre of the market is the focus for about thirty stalls with a particularly roaring trade being done by the stall specialising in Scandinavian Christmas decorations. Most of the things for sale are new, but the nearby charity shop also has a stall and there is a Norwegian run second-hand stall that is a regular at the market. At either end of the marquee, the exposed streets have a unique atmosphere with rows of lights illuminating the winter night.

Visitors hoping to try some traditional Scandinavian food will not be disappointed with all kinds of delicacies from sweet pickles to authentic Swedish meatballs and mash and even reindeer meat sandwiches with lingonberry sauce. Both the Finnish and Norwegian churches offer all kinds of traditional food from freshly made pancakes to hearty fish soups and plenty of seating to relax and enjoy your new culinary experience.

The Christmas market has become a fixture in many Londoners' calendars in the run-up to Christmas, but the spring market is a much more modest affair. The event that takes place here in the early spring has about thirty stalls including local Scandi-artists, a few second-hand stalls and traders offering authentic Swedish, Norwegian and Finnish food. It's a pleasant little market, but nothing to compare with its winter sibling.

Stones Throw Market

St John the Baptist's Church, High Road,
Leytonstone, E11 1HH
www.stonesthrowmarket.co.uk
Twitter/Instagram: @stonesthrowE11

This little pop-up market offers the good folk of Leytonstone a lovely mix of vintage clothing, jewellery, naturally made soaps, unique crockery, recycled wooden homewares and incredible locally produced honey from *Epping Good Honey*. There's also a great little café offering all kinds of homemade cakes. Stones Throw is an occasional market, take a look at their website or social media for the next event.

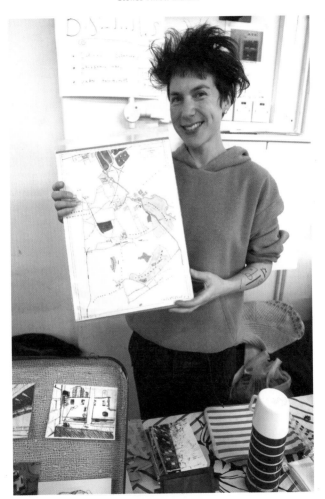

RANK ALDIS
MAGAZINE

Osram
PROJECTOR LAMP
PROJECTOR LAMP
P ... R LAMP
P. Owain R LAMP
PROJECTOR LAMP
PROJECTOR LAMP

WOTAN
WO AN
WOTAN

Birmingham England

ny within t

Aldis - a Company within the Rank Organisation

VINTAGE
FAIRS

Clerkenwell Vintage

www.clerkenwellvintagefashionfair.co.uk
Twitter: @ClerkenwellVint / Instagram: @clerkenwellvint
Freemason's Hall, 60 Great Queen Street, WC2B 5AZ
Clerkenwell Vintage Fair was set up by vintage fashion enthusiast
Savitri Coleman back in 2009 and has since then gained an
international reputation and a loyal following. Started in Clerkenwell,
the Freemason's Hall in the heart of Covent Garden is now the
venue. The fairs are a real celebration of classic style and glamour
with quite a few of the traders and visitors strutting out in their glad
rags and enjoying themselves. If you're looking for an authentic
1940's zoot suit, a raw silk kimono or a 1970's Biba outfit, there's a
good chance you'll find it here.

Clerkenwell Vintage is a monthly event that is well worth
seeking out; once you've been to one you're sure to come back for
more. Take a look at their website for forthcoming events.

Frock Me Vintage

Chelsea Old Town Hall, 161 King's Road, SW3 5EE
or Kensington Town Hall, Hornton Street, W8 7NX
www.frockmevintagefashion.com
Twitter: @frockme / Instagram: @frockmevintage

This bi-monthly vintage clothing fair is one of the trusted features of the vintage calendar with about 70 traders offering all kinds of rare and exquisite garments and accessories. The events are always a lot of fun with crowds of keen vintage shoppers rummaging among the rails and displays to find anything from collectable jewellery to rare kimonos and 1950's dresses.

One of the best things about Frock Me is the regular venue of Chelsea Old Town Hall which provides a fittingly grand environment for the fine threads on show. The event will move to Kensington Town Hall in early 2018 while work is done on the Chelsea venue, but they will return to their old haunt for the autumn. Take a look at their website or social media for the next event.

Hammersmith Vintage Fashion Fair

Hammersmith Town Hall,
1 Riverside Gardens off Kings Street, W6 9JU
www.pa-antiques.co.uk

Established in 1999, this vintage clothing, textiles and accessories fair is an established feature of London's vintage scene. The event's success depends on the great traders that regularly exhibit here, offering all kinds of vintage clothes, jewellery, accessories and textiles with enough discount rails to appeal to vintage bargain hunters.

While many vintage fairs and pop-up events move from venue to venue, this fair has been a permanent fixture on the calendar of Hammersmith Town Hall since 2006. It's a perfect location with the wood panelled main hall providing a fitting backdrop to the carefully displayed vintage wear. The fair takes place about every 6 weeks and is well worth seeking out – take a look at their website for forthcoming events.

Love Vintage

(Wanstead Vintage Fashion & Brocante Fair)
www.lovevintage.co.uk
Twitter: @LoveVintageCary
Held twice a year in June & December

Vintage enthusiast, Cary Whitley, held her first Love Vintage event back in 2010 and since then it has established a great reputation, with 32 of the best vintage traders setting up at this bi-annual event, filling both halls of the fine old Wanstead Church.

Vintage fashionistas will find plenty of things to tempt them with anything from 1940's dresses to some beautifully cut men's suits. Accessories are essential to complete the vintage look and there is always a bewildering choice of vintage jewellery, handbags, ties etc to complete the look. Love Vintage is not just restricted to fashion with plenty of vintage style from a large 1940s chest of drawers to French Brocante pieces. These events only take place twice a year, but that helps keep them special. Take a look at their website or social media for details of forthcoming events.

Pop Up Vintage

www.popupvintagefairs.co.uk
Twitter/Instagram: @Pop_Up_Vintage

Pop Up Vintage Fairs London was founded by fashion enthusiast Maxine Stonehill in 2011 and was voted 'Best London Vintage Fair' for three consecutive years in the Vintage Guide to London Awards. They have since won a place in the hearts of London's vintage hunters. 'Pop Up' is an appropriate name, as the fairs takes place about once a month at a number of grand venues across the city including Wilton's Music Hall, St Stephen's Hampstead, Walthamstow Assembly Hall and Alexandra Palace.

The great thing about the Alexandra Palace event is that it runs alongside a large antiques and collectables fair in the vast Great Hall. There's a different vibe to the two fairs with the fashionable Pop Up crowd rubbing shoulders with antique enthusiasts looking for anything from train memorabilia to antique clocks. Of course there's some cross over with Pop Up Vintage Fairs' traders selling everything from vintage fashion to mid-century retro homeware so there is something for everyone to enjoy!

Whichever Pop Up event you chose, you're sure to have a great time and find some of the best vintage traders and the kind of glamorous customers that seem to be a walking advertisement for the retro lifestyle. Take a look at their website to find out about forthcoming events.

So Last Century

www.solastcenturyfair.co.uk
Twitter/Instagram: @solastc
Monthly events across south London
(Catford, Beckenham and Tooting)

Established by friends Alan Old and Alison Davis in 2015, the wittily-named So Last Century has gained a reputation for organised, friendly events that are always well publicised and attract a good number of south London's vintage-loving community. What sets these fairs apart is the emphasis on reasonably priced vintage goods from homeware to fashion. You'll find lamps, artwork and furniture with lots of original 20th century design on display for a fraction of the price of high-end vintage stores. Among the recent bargains was a fantastic Marcel Breuer style leather and steel armchair for just £130 and a beautiful wooden train and carriages for £35. The regular vintage art and print seller is worth seeking out with his great stock and bespoke framing service. There are a number of vintage fashion specialists with large ranges of well chosen stock, so fashionistas will not be disappointed and many of the other traders also sell good quality, affordable jewellery and accessories. The fair also features a clutch of original designer-makers and artists

So Last Century takes place at a number of venues across south London, with St Dunstan's College in Catford being the largest. Whichever one you attend you're bound to have a great time and there is always a good in-house café to enjoy a break and admire your latest purchases. Take a look at their website for forthcoming events.

CAR BOOT
SALES

Car Boot Sales

NORTH

Classic Car Boot Sale
(see full review on p. 333)

Crouch End Car Boot Sale
Weston Park School
Denton Road, N8 9WP
Twitter: @CECarBoot
Facebook/crouchendcarboot
An occasional car boot sale to raise
funds for Weston Park School.
Take a look at their social media
for forthcoming events.

Holloway Car Boot Sale
Holloway Road, opposite Holloway
Odeon Cinema, N7 6LJ
Tel: 01992 717 198
100 pitches
Sat 8am-4pm, Sun 10am-2.30pm
This long established car boot
sale is a favourite with the locals
offering a wide selection of both
new household goods, clothing,
toys and phone accessories as well
as a great selection of second-
hand gear. The atmosphere is
friendly and even on rainy days
enough people show up to make
this a fun place to have a potter.
If you want to do some standard
grocery shopping while you're out
and about, the great value Nag's
Head Market is just the other side
of Seven Sister's Road.

Caliber Car Boot Sale
St Augustine's School, Kilburn Park
Road, North Maida Vale, NW6 5SN
www.thelondoncarbootco.co.uk
Tel: 07956 312 131
Sat 11am-3pm
Kilburn's car boot sale has been
going for donkey's years and is a
firm favourite with the locals of
NW6. About 60 sellers set up here
on a Saturday selling anything from
a vintage wireless radio to cheap
phone accessories. There are
always bargains to be found here
with recent discoveries including a
top quality iron pan for just a few
quid, an expensive Ortlieb pannier
for just a fiver and mountains of
clothing to sift through for fashion
bargains costing just pennies. The
atmosphere is friendly with lots
of characters more than willing to
have a chat and a laugh and there
is a great café within the school
building if you get peckish.

Stoke Newington Car Boot Sale

Princess May School, Stoke Newington Road, N16 8DF
www.thelondoncarbootco.co.uk
Tel: 07956 312 131
Entry: 7am-9am £3; 9am-2pm 50p
Sat and Sun 7am-3pm

Stoke Newington is now an expensive place to live and this car boot reflects the clientele with a good book and record dealer and several stalls offering fine collectables among the usual array of discarded household goods and piles of old clothes to sift through. Towards the back of the school there are quite a few more organised sellers of vintage and second-hand clothing with some great deals to be found. There are lots of great eateries on Stoke Newington Road if you get peckish, but the organisers also run a tasty little café serving large mugs of tea and sausage sandwiches. If you visit on a Saturday, don't miss the Growing Communities Farmers' Market (see page 279), which is just five minutes away.

Tottenham Car Boot Sale

Tottenham Community Sports Centre, Tottenham High Road, N17 8AD
www.countrysidepromotions.co.uk
Tel: 01992 468 619
55 pitches
Thurs 6am-2pm

WEST

Chiswick Car Boot Sale

Chiswick School,
Burlington Lane, W4 3UN
Tel: 020 8747 0031
www.chiswickschool.org
200 pitches
First Sun of month (except Jan) 8am-1pm (set up from 7am)

SOUTH

Battersea Boot

Battersea Park School
401 Battersea Park Road, SW11 5AP
www.batterseaboot.com
Tel: 07941 383 588
250 pitches
Sun 1.30-5pm

Capital Car Boot Sale

Pimlico Academy
St Lupus Street, SW1V 3AT
www.capitalcarboot.com
Tel: 07376 886 379
Entry £1 / Early Bird (10.15) £5
Sun 11.30am-2.30pm

Meridian Boot Sale Charlton

Charlton Lane, SE7 8QS
Pitches 150
Tel: 020 8856 1923
Pitches 50-70
Entry: free
Sat 7.30am-12.30pm

New Covent Garden Car Boot Sale

*Nine Elms Lane,
Battersea, SW8 5AL
www.saundersmarkets.co.uk
Tel: 01483 277 640
150 pitches
Sun 6am-2pm*

Located in the concrete and steel landscape of New Covent Garden Market, and managed by Saunders Markets Ltd on behalf of New Covent Garden Authority, this car boot sale is one of the biggest and best in the capital. It also takes place at the same time as the Vauxhall Sunday Market and it's difficult to know where one ends and the other begins, which only adds to the fun. The place is packed on a Sunday and is very popular with London's eastern European and African communities who wander the aisles in search of bargains. There are a few things to note when visiting here: if you buy a bike you'll need to cycle it home as London Transport won't allow it on the tube and because this is a fruit and veg wholesale market in the week, dogs are not allowed. These restrictions apart, this is one of the best things to do on a Sunday in west London and while most car boot sales offer basic British grub, here you can find anything from paella to curry.

EAST

Picks Cottage Car Boot Sale

Picks Cottage, Sewardstone Road
Waltham Abbey, E4 7RA
www.pickscottage.co.uk
Tel: 020 8529 3922
Sun 6.30am-1.30pm

OUT OF TOWN

Bishop Stortford Boot Sale

Train Station Car Park,
Anchor Street, CM23 3BP
www.countrysidepromotions.co.uk
Tel: 01992 468 619
Pitches 150
Sun (March-Oct) 11.30am-3pm

Boreham Car Boot Sale

General Farm (A12), Boreham,
Essex, CM3 3HJ
www.countrygroupevents.co.uk
Tel: 07779 948 946
Sun (March-November) 6am-2pm

Chigwell Rise Boot Sale

Chigwell Rise nr David Lloyd Center,
Essex, IG7 6AB
www.countrygroupevents.co.uk
Tel: 07779 948 946
Sat (April-May and Sept-Oct) 6am-2pm

Denham Giant Car Boot

Main A40 Denham Roundabout,
UB9 5PG
www.giantcarboot.co.uk
Tel: 07947 121 336
Entry £2, £1 (after 11am)
Sat 9am-3pm

Often called Uxbridge Car Boot, this is one of the biggest car boots in the south east and well worth making an effort to visit with hundreds of pitches.

Flamingo Park Car Boot Sale

A20 Sidcup By Pass, Chislehurst,
Kent, BR7 6HL
www.flamingopark.co.uk
Tel: 020 8309 1012
300 pitches
Sun (April-Aug) 9am-3pm

Harlow Car Boot Sale

Barrows Road Car Park, Pinnacles
Industrial Estate,
Harlow, CM19 5FA
www.countrysidepromotions.co.uk
Tel: 01992 468 619
300 pitches
Sun 10.30am-3pm

Hayes Street Farm Car Boot

239 Hayes Lane, Bromley, Kent,
BR2 7LB
www.hayessfarm.co.uk
Twitter: HayesStreetFarm
Tel: 020 8462 1186
Entry: 50p
Fortnightly Sundays April-Sept
6am-3pm

Hounslow Heath Car Boot

Hounslow Heath Garden Centre,
Staines Road, Middlesex,
TW4 5DL
www.hounslowheathcarboot.co.uk
Tel: 07891 265 124
Entry: £1, early bird (before
8.30am) £2
Thurs, Sun and Bank Holiday Mon
8.30am-3pm

North Weald Car Boot

North Weald Airfield, Merlin Way,
CM16 6HR
www.saundersmarkets.co.uk
Tel: 01483 277 640
Pitches 150
Entry: free
Sat 8am-3pm

This is one of the largest and best car boots and has the advantage of running parallel with a large market offering all kinds of great value food, household goods and new clothing. It's just 20 minutes north up the M11 from Redbridge Roundabout and easily reached if you're coming from east London.

Redbourn Boot Sale

Herts Showground, Dunstable Road,
Herts, AL3 7PT
www.countrysidepromotions.co.uk
Tel: 01992 468 619
300 Pitches
Sun (April-Oct) 10.30am-3pm

Shepperton Boot Sale

New Road, Shepperton,
Surrey, TW17 0QC
www.sheppertoncarboot.co.uk
Tel: 07807 609 283
Entry: £1 / Early Birds
(Before 8.30am) £3
Sun 7.30am-1.30pm

Sutton Car Boot

Opposite St Heller Hospital
Wrythe Lane, Sutton,
Surrey, SM5 1AA
www.Suttoncarboot.co.uk
Tel: 07459 539 439
Wed 8am-1pm

Waltham Abbey Boot Sale

Netherhouse Farm, Sewardstone
Road, Essex, E4 7RJ
www.countrysidepromotions.co.uk
Tel: 01992 468 619
Sun (July-Oct) 10.30am-2pm

Welwyn Car Boot Sale

Stanborough Park, North Car Park,
Stanborough Road, AL8 6FX
www.countrysidepromotions.co.uk
Tel: 01992 468 619
100 pitches
Sun (April-Nov)10am-2pm

FARMERS' MARKETS

20 YEARS
OF FARMERS MARKETS
IN LONDON

LONDON
FARMERS
MARKETS

WWW.LFM.ORG.UK

Farmers' Markets

Farmers' Markets

The concept of Farmers' Markets, where local food producers sell direct to the public, has been one of America's more benign exports. In the last twenty years this type of market has proved a great success in London, providing a lifeline for many small independent farmers who were previously struggling to survive.

London's Farmers' Markets (LFM) was the pioneer in the field and still runs the largest number of farmers' markets in the capital, applying strict rules to ensure that only genuine farmers – no food distributors – sell at their markets. A later arrival on the scene is City & Country Farmers' Markets, which has a less strict criteria for stall holders and runs several markets that are of wider appeal (Herne Hill and Alexandra Palace) and merit their own reviews within this book.

London has also proved fertile soil for a number of successful independent farmers' markets which have flourished with a local management team and the loyal support of the surrounding community, and these quirky independents are all featured. We've also included the Food Assembly which is a scheme using technology to allow consumers to order direct from food producers.

Farmers' Markets are concerned with all kinds of praiseworthy issues such as sustainability, reducing food miles and improving the connection between food producers and consumers, but above all they are a lot of fun and a great way to enjoy the process of getting your groceries.

London Farmers' Markets

www.lfm.org.uk
info@lfm.org.uk
Twitter: @londonfarmers
Instagram: londonfarmers

London Farmers' Markets (LFM) were the pioneers of the concept of farmers markets in the UK, having set up their first market in Islington in 1999. The organisation now runs more than 20 weekly markets, putting foodies across London in contact with over 200 farmers and their produce. The concept of a farmers' market might sound a little dry and worthy, but the markets are a lot of fun with street food, plenty of delicious cakes and breads and a fair number of deli and specialist food stalls all part of the mix.

Their long running Saturday market on Bute Street in the heart of Kensington is a great example of a LFM event as it features handcrafted goat's cheese from *Windrush Valley*, *Parsons Nose* cooking up a storm with delicious sausages and burgers, *Winterbourne Game* for the kind of meats you won't find in the supermarkets, plus several seasonal fruit and veg stalls.

Bute Street always has a good choice of prepared foods with several traders offering cakes, pastries and artisanal breads, an Italian stall selling jars of pesto and fresh pasta and a London based distillery offering their own brand of Gin. The market also boasts a very popular fish stall with a wonderful selection of fish and shellfish. London Farmers' Markets all have their own unique atmosphere and Bute Street has a gallic feel with a large French community in the area, but the quality and variety of food is always high. Below are all the London Farmers' Markets running across the capital, but always check their informative website for updates and forthcoming events.

Balham
Henry Cavendish Primary School,
Hydethorpe Road, SW12 0JA
Open: Saturday 9am-1pm

Blackheath
Blackheath Rail Station Car Park,
2 Blackheath Village, SE3 9LA
Open: Sunday 10am-2pm

Bloomsbury
Torrington Square, Byng Place,
Behind ULU, WC1E 7HY
Open: Thursday 9am-2pm

Ealing
Leeland Road,
West Ealing, W13 9HH
Open: Saturday 9am-1pm

Earls Court
St Cuthbert with Matthias School,
Warwick Road, SW5 9UE
Open: Sunday 10am-2pm

Islington
Chapel Market,
Between Penton St
and Baron St, N1 9PZ
Open: Sunday 10am-2pm

London Bridge
King's College London, Guys
Campus, SE1 1UL
Open: Tuesday 9am-2pm

Marylebone
Cramer Street Car Park,
Corner Moxon Street, W1U 4EW
Open: Sunday 10am-2pm

Notting Hill
Car Park behind Waterstones
Kensington Church St, W11 3LQ
Open: Saturday 9am-1pm

Parliament Hill
Entrance on the heath tennis
courts, William Ellis School, off
Highgate Road, NW5 1RN
Open: Saturday 10am-2pm

Parson's Green
Thomas's Academy, New King's
Road, Opposite Cristowe Road,
SW6 4LY
Open: Sunday 10am-2pm

Pimlico Road
Orange Square, corner of Pimlico
Road & Ebury Street, SW1W 8UT
Open: Saturday 9am-1pm

Queen's Park
Salusbury Primary School,
Salusbury Road, NW6 6RG
Open: Sunday 10am-2pm

Ransome's Dock
Nutbourne Restaurant Yard,
Ransome's Dock. Parkgate Road,
Battersea Park, SW11 4NP
Open: Saturday 10am-2pm

South Kensington (Saturday)
Bute Street, Kensington, SW7 3EX
Open: Saturday 9am-2pm

South Kensington (Tuesdays)
Queens Lawn, Imperial College,
SW7 5NH
Open: Tuesday 9am-2pm

Swiss Cottage
Eton Avenue, off Finchley Road,
NW3 3EU
Open: Wednesday 10am-3pm

Twickenham
Holly Road Car Park,
Holly Road (off King Street),
TW1 4HF
Open: Saturday 9am-1pm

Walthamstow
Town Square by Selbourne
Walk Shopping Centre, off the
High Street, E17 7JN
Open: Sunday 10am-2pm

West Hampstead
West Hampstead Thameslink
Station Forecourt,
Iverson Rd, NW6 1PF
Open: Saturday 10am-2pm

Westminster Bridge
St Thomas' Hospital Gardens,
Westminster Bridge Rd, SE1 7EP
Open: Thursday 10am-3pm

Wimbledon
Wimbledon Park First School,
Havana Road,
off Durnsford Road, SW19 8EJ
Open: Saturday 9am-1pm

City & Country Farmers' Markets

Oval Farmers' Market

St Mark's Church, The Oval, SE11 4PW
www.weareccfm.com
Twitter: @weareccfm
Open: Saturday 10am-3pm

Every Saturday the grounds of St Mark's Church are given over to this popular farmers' market. The church yard is right next to the busy A3 and within a stone's throw of The Oval cricket ground, but on fine days it has something of the atmosphere of a village fête, with visitors lounging on the grass or strolling among the avenue of about 40 stalls.

It's a great place for the good folk of Kennington to do their weekly shop with a great fishmongers, several bread and pastry stalls and a number of pitches offering seasonal fruit and veg straight from the farm. Top quality and ethically-produced meat can be found from the likes of *Grove Farm* and *Marsh Produce* and there are also several stalls offering prepared deli produce with anything from cured and hand-carved Iberian ham to a stall specialising in a bewildering array of olives.

The street food stalls are also very popular here with anything from *Giggly Pig's* sausage sandwiches (they also sell their sausages to take home) to vegan salad boxes and another stall offering fishy treats like squid and chips. The market also boasts an excellent coffee stall, providing a delicious caffeine fix to round off a visit to this great little farmers' market.

Other City & Country Farmers' Markets

Alexandra Palace (see page 61)
Herne Hill (see page 225)

Lewisham
Telegraph Hill, Erlander Road & Arbuthnot Road, SE14 5LS
& Manor House Gardens, Old Road entrance, SE13 5SY
Twitter: @lewishamfm
Open: Fortnightly Saturday 10am-3pm
City & Country run two fortnightly farmers' markets in the
Lewisham area. Check their website or Twitter for details.

Stepney
Stepney City Farm, Stepney Way, E1 3DG
Twitter: @stepneyfm
Open: Saturday 10am-3pm

Barnes Farmers' Market

Essex House Surgery, SW13 0LW
www.barnesfarmersmarket.co.uk
Rail: Barnes Bridge
Open: Saturday 10am-2pm

This independent farmers' market occupies the car park of
Essex House Surgery, just opposite the Barnes Duck Pond, every
Saturday. It's one of the first farmers' markets, having been
around for nearly 20 years, with many of the original traders still
offering the good folk of Barnes the chance to buy direct from
the farmer and food producer. Expect to find delicious breads
and cakes, organic and free range meat, cured meats, hams and
sausages, freshly made pastas, artisan cheeses, seasonal fruit and
veg, as well as fresh fish from the *Portland Scallop Company*. This
might not be your local market, but it's worth making a bit of a
trek to visit – if only enjoy the village atmosphere of Barnes.

Brook Green Farmers' Market

Addison Primary School, Bolingbroke Road, W14 0DT
www.brookgreenmarket.co.uk
Twitter: @brookgreen_mk
Tube: Shepherd's Bush or Goldhawk Road
Open: Saturday 10am-3pm

This independent FARMA certified farmers' market has won a
place in the hearts of the locals of Shepherd's Bush. Every Saturday
morning about 25 independent food producers descend on this
school playground, transforming it into an oasis of fresh produce,
prepared dishes, street foods and various specialist beers and
wines. Visitors can expect to find artisan breads and cakes from
the likes of *Aston's Bakery*, several cheesemongers, quality and
ethically produced meat and a great choice of seasonal fruit and
veg direct from the farm. Among the other delicacies to look out

for are freshly prepared pasta and a selection of deli stalls offering anything from marinated olives to cured meats.

The market also has a great choice of street food with established names like *Gyoza Guys*, *Biff's Jack Shack* and *Lords of Poké* all among the regulars here. If you need a caffeine fix look out for the mobile barista – *Scotties Coffee*.

The market organisers keep things fresh with a busy programme of themed events, live music, cookery talks and demos, and even boardgames. To find out more about the market take a look at their website and subscribe to their newsletter.

Horniman Farmers' Market

Bandstand Terrace, Horniman Museum Gardens,
100 London Road, SE23 3PQ
www.horniman.ac.uk
Twitter: @HornimanFarmers
Rail: Forest Hill
Open: Every Saturday 9am – 1.30pm

The Horniman Museum is one of London's most interesting venues with a fascinating anthropological archive and collection of musical instruments. On Saturdays the garden of the museum transforms itself into a very different anthropological experiment as the foodies of Southeast London congregate to source delicious essentials directly from independent, local producers.

It's a great location and now attracts stalls selling seasonal fruit and vegetables, artisan organic bread, cakes, cheese, pies, scotch eggs, freshly squeezed juices, herbal infusions, organic meat, salads and herbs. On intermittent weeks you will also find free-range salami and handcrafted, ethically made chocolates plus other guest stalls selling craft beer, preserves, kimchi and plants. There are also some street food stalls offering anything from falafel to crêpes – the surrounding gardens are a wonderful place to enjoy a picnic.

Other Farmers' Markets:

There are several markets that have been included in other
parts of this book, but could equally well be included here:

Alexandra Palace Farmers' Market (see page 61)
Primrose Hill Farmers' Market (see page 105)
Tottenham Green (see page 119)
Brockley (see page 197)
Crystal Palace Food Market (see page 201)
Herne Hill Farmers' Market (see page 225)
Growing Communities (see page 279)
London Fields Sunday Market (see page 289)

The Food Assembly

www.thefoodassembly.com
Twitter: @foodassembly
Instagram: foodassembly
support@thefoodassembly.com

The Food Assembly is a social and collaborative enterprise
which puts consumers in contact with food producers. Put
simply, you register on line, join your local assembly, order
and pay for your groceries from a range of local producers
and then collect at a nearby assembly market. There are 16
food assembly points in London, so Londoners have a great
opportunity to participate in the scheme.

WEEK AT A GLANCE

CENTRAL

	M	T	W	T	F	S	S
Berwick Street	•	•	•	•	•	•	
Cabbages & Frocks						•	
Charing Cross Collectors Fair							•
Covent Garden	❶	❹	❹	❹	❹	❹	
Earlham Street	•	•	•	•	•	•	
KERB Gherkin				L			
Leather Lane	L	L	L	L	L		
Lower Marsh Street	•	•	•	•	•	•	
Piccadilly Market	•	•	❹	❹	❹	❹	
Smithfield	*	*	*	*	*		
Southbank Book Market	❷	❷	❷	❷	❷	❷	❷
Southbank Centre Food Market					•	•	•
Street Food Union @Rupert Street	L	L	L	L	L		
Tachbrook Street				L	L	L	
Whitecross Street	L	L	L	L	L		

NORTH

	M	T	W	T	F	S	S
Alexandra Palace Farmers' Market							•
Alfies Antiques Market		❶	❶	❶	❶	❶	
Archway Market						•	
Camden Market	<	<	<	•	•	•	•
Camden Passage			❶	❷		❶	❶
Chalton Street			•	•	•	•	
Chaple Market			•	•	•	•	•
Church Street			•	•	•	•	
Hampstead Community Market	<	<	<	<	<	•	<
Hoxton Street	<	<	<	<	<	•	
Inverness Street	•	•	•	•	•	•	•
KERB King's Cross			L	L	L		
Kilburn Square	•	•	•	•	•	•	
Nag's Head	•	•	•	•	•	•	❸
Primrose Hill Farmers' Market						L	
Queen's Crescent				>		•	
Stroud Green							L
Swiss Cottage			•		•	•	

384

	M	T	W	T	F	S	S
Tottenham Green							•
Bayswater Road Art Exhibition							•
Duck Pond Market Richmond						•	❹
Duck Pond Market Ruislip							•
North End Road	•	•	•		•	•	
Partridges Food Market						•	
Portobello	<	<	<	>	<	•	<
Shepherd's Bush	•	•	•		•	•	

SOUTHWEST

	M	T	W	T	F	S	S
Brixton	•	•	>	•	•	•	
Broadway & Tooting Markets		•	•	>	•	•	•
Hildreth Street	•	•	>	•	•	•	
Northcote Road	•	•	>	•	•	•	
Northcote Road Antiques Market	•	•	•	•	•	•	>
Putney Market						L	
Vauxhall Sunday Market							•
Venn Street						•	

SOUTHEAST

	M	T	W	T	F	S	S
Bermondsey Antiques Market				>			
Borough Market	<	<	•	•	•	•	
Brockley						L	
Crystal Palace Food Market							•
Deptford			•		•	•	
East Street		•	•	•	•	•	
Elephant & Castle	•	•	•	•	•	•	
Flea @ Flat Iron Square						•	•
Greenwich Market	<	<	<	<	<	•	•
Clock Tower Market						•	•
Haynes Lane						•	•
Herne Hill Farmers' Market							•
Lewisham High Street	•	•	•	•	•	•	•
Maltby Street						•	•
North Cross Road						•	
West Norwood Feast (monthly)							•

EAST

	M	T	W	T	F	S	S
Bethnal Green Road	•	•	•	>	•	•	
Billingsgate		*	*	*	*	*	
Brick Lane				<	<	•	•
Broadway Market					•		
Broadway Vegan Market					•		
Chatsworth Road							
Chrisp Street	•	•	•	•	•	•	
Columbia Road							•
E17 Village Market					•		
Growing Communities					•		
Hackney Downs Vegan Market							•
Kingsland Waste					•		
Limehouse Social (monthly)							•
London Fields Sunday Market							•
Netil Market					•		
Petticoat Lane	<	<	<	<	<	•	
Queen's Market		•		•	•	•	
Ridley Road	•	•	•	•	•	•	
Roman Road		•		•	•	•	
Spitalfields	•	•	•	①	•	•	•
Victoria Park							•
Walthamstow	•	•	•	•	•	•	•
Well Street (monthly)					•		
Whitechapel Market	•	•	•	>	•	•	

KEY

- •   Open all day
- >   Open half-day
- L   Lunchtime markets
- <   Market partially open
- *   Open early mornings only

- ①   Antiques Market
- ②   Book Market
- ③   Bric-à-brac
- ④   Arts & Crafts

INDEX

Index

About us:

Metro is a small independent publishing company with a reputation for producing well-researched and beautifully-designed guides on many aspects of London life.

In fields of interest as diverse as shopping, bargain hunting, architecture, the arts, and food, our guide books contain special tips you won't find anywhere else.

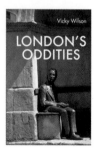

www.metropublications.com

London's Hidden Walks Series

LONDON'S HIDDEN WALKS
THE LONDON WE KNOW IS JUST THE SURFACE!
Volume 1

LONDON'S HIDDEN WALKS
EXPLORE LONDON AND DISCOVER HOW 2000 YEARS OF HISTORY HAVE SHAPED THIS CITY
Volume 2

LONDON'S HIDDEN WALKS
WALK, EXPLORE, DISCOVER...
Volume 3

LONDON'S CITY CHURCHES
SEE THE SCORCH MARKS OF THE GREAT FIRE, OR VISIT AN ALTAR BY HENRY MOORE

LONDON'S HOUSES
FROM WORKHOUSE TO ROYAL PALACE, COME IN, CLOSE THE DOOR AND STEP BACK IN TIME...

LONDON'S MONUMENTS
FROM BOUDICCA AND BYRON TO GUY THE GORILLA

LONDON'S PARKS AND GARDENS
COVER MORE THAN TWENTY-FIVE PERCENT OF THE CAPITAL – THAT'S A LOT MORE GRASS BETWEEN TOES THAN ANY OTHER CITY IN EUROPE

LONDON'S CEMETERIES
SPEND THE DAY WITH KARL MARX, ENID BLYTON, KEITH MOON AND MANY MORE

EDINBURGH'S HIDDEN WALKS
WALK, EXPLORE, DISCOVER...

Market Map